THE GREAT SERPENT MOUND

THE GREAT SERPENT MOUND

AN ANCIENT OHIO MYSTERY

JEFFREY ALAN JOHN, PHD

Published by The History Press
An imprint of Arcadia Publishing
Charleston, SC
www.historypress.com

First published 2025

Manufactured in the United States

ISBN 9781467159708
Hardcover ISBN 9781540299871

Library of Congress Control Number: 2025941144

Notice: The information in this book is true and complete to the best of our knowledge. It is offered without guarantee on the part of the author or The History Press. The author and The History Press disclaim all liability in connection with the use of this book.

CONTENTS

ACKNOWLEDGEMENTS

The journey toward this book began several years ago, when as tourists my wife, Karin, and I visited Serpent Mound State Memorial. I knew the effigy well because the Ohio History Connection maintains the site; decades ago, as a public relations writer for what was then known as the Ohio Historical Society, I had written about it often. Today, differences of opinion swirl around the site, and the proliferation of beliefs stimulated my curiosity. Who really made Serpent Mound, and why?

This book can't fill the gaps in space and time definitively, but I have been able to assemble learned discussions with the help of many people I've met along the way. Beth Jenkins, site manager for Serpent Mound State Memorial, deserves special mention because she has answered all my questions with fairness and honesty. She knows a thing or two about the site, and she can point the direction toward sources of information for what she doesn't know.

Another great source has been Bradley Lepper, PhD, the chief archaeologist for the Ohio History Connection. Brad's science-based theories about the origins and age of Serpent Mound have placed a target squarely on his own back, but his writing builds a strong defense. I thank him for his time and cooperation in preparation of this book.

Barbara Alice Mann, PhD, of the University of Toledo, Ohio, doesn't always agree with Dr. Lepper, but she supplied a great deal of in-depth information related to Native Americans and the mythology of the Great Horned Serpent.

Two colleagues from my institution, Wright State University, shared their time and knowledge. Geologist David Schmidt, PhD, met me for a fascinating conversation about the effects of the object that created the ancient crater where Serpent Mound was built, and archaeologist Robert Reardon, PhD, described his experiences as one of the top researchers studying Ohio's prehistoric cultures.

When I sought the identity of the first nonnative people who might have seen the effigy in historic times, I found a considerable array of names. Hundreds of early settlers descended on Adams County as soon as Ohio became a state in 1803, and they are remembered in careful lists in the Adams County Recorder's Office, where Angie Caraway generously shared her time to offer guidance and direction.

Perhaps the most detailed information about the original white settlers of the land on which Serpent Mound sits came from Delsey Wilson. Mrs. Wilson, a longtime resident of Adams County and a local historian, graciously shared her knowledge and provided directions to a county newsletter article she had written that describes in detail the lineage of all the white owners of the property in historical times.

This book could not have been written without access to dozens, if not hundreds, of archives and records. Ohio's premier (and official) document collections are held by the Ohio History Connection, where Connie Connor found and provided for me boxes, folders, books and documents. I can't thank her and the hardworking OHC archives and library staff enough for repeatedly hauling carts full of heavy, dusty boxes and folders down from stacks on the upper floors of their building so I could examine them.

As the journey toward publishing this book nears its completion, I must thank publisher's representative Joe Gartrell. Joe has been a cooperative and helpful guide through many steps along the way.

My constant companion on this journey has been Karin Avila-John. She prompts and encourages through the long process and willingly accompanied me on many tours to earthworks and effigies throughout southern Ohio (although I was warned not to make such a tour the centerpiece of our fortieth wedding anniversary). I cannot do without you.

PROLOGUE

Some 300 million years ago, reptiles the size and shape of squat English bulldogs scuttled along the flat plains of the continent Pangea. A few steps ahead of the larger animals, tiny shrew-like proto-mammals kicked up dust, trying to burrow underground to escape being eaten. Around these beasts a few ferns sprouted from thick stalks, but they were hardly enough to color the barren landscape. During the day, sun baked the soil and repelled most moving things, while in the evenings the air cooled enough to encourage small creatures out into the open. Compared to today, the land that would eventually become North America was not a pleasant environment.[1]

One evening, points of bright light streaked out of the dark sky. Living creatures barely had time to look up and try to scamper away before one of the sparks expanded suddenly, igniting the air and detonating in a blinding light. With a roar greater than anything the beasts had ever heard, a solid mass blotted out most of the sky and smashed the Earth.

The impact transformed rock of the formerly barren plains to a depth of about a half mile. The hurtling concretion liquified and shoved aside formerly level limestone layers, heaving them up into near-vertical walls around a circle nine miles wide, while it altered the magnetic properties of some of the rock.[2] Unmeasurable atmospheric forces in the middle of the giant dish splashed fluid rock into an enormous peak, while an instant after the impact a firestorm scorched everything as far as could be seen and beyond. Boulders with the mass of small hills, heaved up by the explosion, rained down amid debris that eventually measured one thousand feet thick. On the distant horizon, living creatures felt the ground shake violently.[3]

The impact launched an enormous dust cloud into the atmosphere. Winds dissipated the dust and filtered the sun's rays so that within days, strange aerial colors enveloped the entire arc of the planet. For about a year, weather patterns changed, but this was a mere blip in the long stretch of the planet Earth's environmental history. Over time, the single Pangea land mass broke up, inland oceans formed and retreated and constant wind and rain softened the edges of the giant crater. When human beings eventually arrived, they stood on high ground and scanned what appeared to be a valley that stretched as far as they could see.

Chapter 1

A BURIAL

Clan leaders and priests had come upon a clearing at the top of a hill with a beautiful view of the valley below, and one of them even said the place "felt" different, but now Akikta wished they had chosen some place lower in the valley. Every footfall stabbed him with more pain as he trudged up the slope. The basket full of earth seemed to grow so heavy that when he reached the top, it greatly relieved Akikta to dump the soil at the feet of the priests directing him. He could see the effigy already beginning to take shape, but on this day he didn't care. Exhausted and ill, he flopped down on the portion of the slope that he had been building. His wife, Shisi, who had carried her basket in the line just behind him, knelt next to Akikta and put a gentle hand on his face. "You look terrible," she said. "Let me help you down to our place."

Yesterday he had felt fine when he, as one of the grown men of the clan, joined in a successful hunt. He recalled how he and a small group of armed friends had laughed and gossiped as they tiptoed through the forest, and Akikta didn't know what to think of the rumor one of the men relayed. It seemed a traveling party from the direction of the rising sun passed along stories they had heard about strange big boats on a huge endless water, carrying blue-eyed men with light hair. Just another fanciful story, Akikta thought, but what if the rumor was true?

The hunters had been out barely any time at all when their scout spotted a large antlered deer close enough to stalk easily. The group followed the usual strategy, and within a short time they had cornered and downed the big beast. It had not succumbed yet, however, and lay thrashing on the forest floor when Akikta and a couple others approached. Then one of the deer's hind legs lashed out, its hoof striking Akikta just below his ribs. It hit him hard enough to fling him backward into a sitting position; when he recovered and staggered to his feet, everyone had a good laugh.

They also had a good catch, and since it was still early evening, the hunters were able to return triumphant with a trophy large enough to support the clan with food for days. First, though, the catch provided meat for a fine dinner that night. Everyone enjoyed it except Akikta, who wasn't hungry but rather bent and aching. Eventually, he made his excuses and stumbled off to his bed, but he got no rest. The tea Shisi brought helped only a little, and despite its warmth, he shivered and perspired all night. By the time of dawn's rising light, Akikta was miserable, but after some more tea and a thin porridge, swallowed at his wife's insistence, he felt obligated to help haul dirt to make the monument.

After carrying only the one basket, Akikta left the work, mostly supported by his son and one of his brothers, and crawled into his bed. The sweet fumes of campfire smoke filled his nostrils as Akikta struggled to know where he was; eventually he drifted out of consciousness. He awoke a couple times during the next day, and when the members of the clan who knew something about ailments visited, touched him and consulted with Shisi, Akikta vaguely recognized them. A day later, his breath came with much greater difficulty, and when he tried to speak, he could make only sounds.

As the sun set that day, his wife heard him murmur something, his lungs heaved and then they were still. Sobbing, Shisi called the priests, friends and others of the community into the lodge where her husband lay. Fires, chants and a little dancing followed; Akikta had not been a major community leader, but as one of the senior men of the group, he had been respected. Thus, the clan elders, in consultation with his wife, began to prepare his path into the afterlife.

There were burial monuments nearby, left by ancestors long gone. As in other places with these monuments, the priests of the clan community felt it appropriate to continue to use these burial places. Shisi picked one near their current effigy project, a nice spot with trees and a view of the Great Serpent they were building, and the elders carefully scratched out a ledge in the little hill. They placed his favorite pipe, some treasured ornaments and his most favored shoes in the indentation. Then, following custom, they built a large fire, and when it had burned down to hot coals, Akikta's family placed his body on it. They quickly spread earth over the resting spot; through the next seasons, Shisi, Akikta's son and daughter and brothers tended to the site as the ground settled. By the time work on the serpent monument was completed, grass and a sapling tree had sprouted at the burial. Eventually the clan moved on, leaving only memories to tell where lay the body of Akikta the hunter, family man and respected member of the clan.

Chapter 2

EUROPEAN DISCOVERY

Three boys stumbling along the north bank of the Ohio River in the summer of 1846 wanted only a couple smooth little stones to use for sinkers on their fishing lines. They found instead an artifact of history: an inscribed lead plate tangled in elm tree roots that had been exposed by river currents. The boys, sons of prominent citizens of Point Pleasant, Ohio, extracted the plate and took it to James Beale, a former member of Congress who had moved to the area. Beale, in turn, delivered the legal pad–sized plate to scholars who concluded it was one of several such markers buried one hundred years earlier by Pierre-Joseph Celeron de Bienville as testimony of French ownership of the Ohio lands.[4] The marker was all that remained of some of the earliest European explorations of the territory.

By the time the boys found the marker in the mid-nineteenth century, the United States of America had absorbed Ohio as its seventeenth state. The territory had become busy and industrious, interlaced with canals and paved roads that connected its more than 1.5 million citizens. Native peoples who once lived and hunted there had been mostly pushed aside, leaving behind a puzzling array of earthen mounds and effigies. Questioned by whites who investigated the formations, Indigenous people feigned ignorance of the origin and purpose of the earthen structures.[5]

By the time European explorers and settlers found the mounds, complex earthworks and animal representations throughout the Northwest Territories, all firsthand knowledge of the mound builders had evaporated.[6]

The first Spanish in the New World had imported bubonic plague that wiped out Indigenous groups that may have been descendants of mound builders, and the Iroquois Confederacy, the Five Nations from the East, had helped depopulate the Ohio and Kentucky territories by initiating lengthy, even ancestral, warfare among tribes. As early as the 1600s, the Iroquois acquired firepower from the British and used it to drive out the Algonquin, the Huron, the Miami and the Shawnee. They also attempted to remove despised French claimants to the land.

Those claimants included the French Celeron de Bienville, the captain in the French army who had buried the plates along the Ohio River. He had been ordered into the Ohio Country to confirm French claims on the territory, so in 1749, Celeron and about 250 soldiers marched south from Montreal, Canada, and entered the Ohio River at its origin with the confluence of the Allegheny and Monongahela Rivers. The troop canoed south to the mouth of the Great Miami River near what is now Cincinnati, stopping at six occasions to bury inscribed lead plates claiming ownership, a common European practice. Celeron de Bienville reported encountering British and Native peoples at outposts along the river, exchanging fur for European hardware. These hardy traders ignored French claims to the land.

The British had, in fact, tried to establish claims on the New France empire that had been pressed south from Canada, including lands that became the Ohio Country. Years before Celeron's expedition, Rene Robert Cavelier Sieur La Salle in 1668–69 explored the area after he heard from Indigenous peoples of a great river that flowed to China. His expedition, from Montreal to Lake Ontario, across woodlands to the Ohio River and then south to waterfalls at present-day Louisville, failed to establish that fabled link, but credit has gone to La Salle for being the first European to see the Ohio River, and he introduced the land to French fur traders who established centers of commerce with Native people. Unfortunately, across the Atlantic Ocean France warred with Britain, which set up an embargo on trade goods the French needed to exchange for furs. Thus the French and English existed in a state of conflict until the French and Indian War (1756–63) that ended when the Treaty of Paris (1763) ceded the Ohio Country to Great Britain.

The peace those European treaties crafted did not extend to reality in the Ohio Country. Communities were forced to erect log walls for protection; no settler dared to tend crops outside the walls alone and unarmed, lest he or she fall into the hands of Native people trying to enforce claims to the region. At the same time, marauding bands of whites attacked Native Americans with equal ferocity. As a result, in 1774 Britain formally annexed

Ohio and other western lands to the Province of Quebec and prohibited settlements west of the Appalachians. This incensed would-be settlers in the American colonies and helped encourage the American Revolution.

Results of that conflict forever affected the land of the mounds and earthworks. The defeated English Crown relinquished its claim to the Ohio Country, which the new United States of America absorbed and parceled out among states. Virginia took 6,570 square miles it called the Virginia Military District and used this land as payments to veterans of the Revolution.

That number included Captain Abraham Shepherd, who earned a large parcel in the Virginia Military District through tragic experience. On November 16, 1776, Shepherd commanded a squad of Virginia militia on the island of Manhattan's high ground, with a colonial force of about 3,000 facing 8,000 British and Hessian troops. Despite early success against two Hessian uphill attacks—during which expert Virginia marksman Daniel Bediger earned lasting fame for firing his muzzle-loading rifle twenty-seven times—colonial forces fell back into their fortification known as Fort Washington, where they were surrounded and captured.[7] The British removed the surviving 2,800 colonial combatants to prisons and penal ships so foul that only 800 survived the war,[8] but Captain Shepherd endured to be exchanged on parole in 1778. After the war, Virginia rewarded his valor with one thousand acres of Virginia Military District land.[9]

Shepherd found that he received rolling, heavily wooded, rocky property. It has not been established that he knew his property included earthen mounds and a low, lengthy earthen rise in the shape of a serpent, but neither Shepherd nor his nephews, who purchased the property from him around 1800, made special note of them, nor were the earthworks identified on an atlas of the newly named Adams County in 1814. Yet their existence was no secret: William Pidgeon, an author whose success fed on supposed knowledge of mound builder ancestry, claimed he made a trek to the mound in 1832, at which time he used a crowbar to pry apart a stone altar at the head of a snake.[10] A modern local historian confirms the earthworks' limited fame. "By 1840, Serpent Mound was very well known to the locals," says Delsey Wilson, who compiled a meticulous record of the land's owners.[11] She suggests Abraham Shepherd actually lived about twenty miles away while he sold off parcels of the property; according to Wilson, the first person to actually live on the property and cultivate it was William Hamilton, who probably found the rolling, wooded and rocky property ill-suited for productive farming. In 1841, he sold 160 acres that included the serpent effigy and mounds to James P. Lovett.

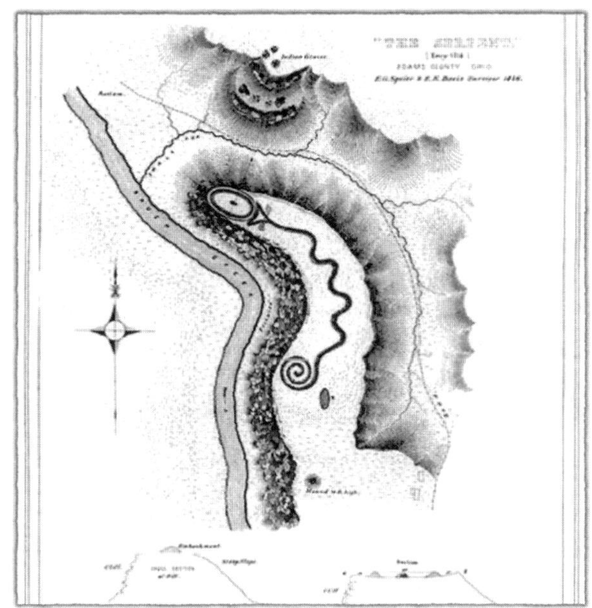

Etching of the Serpent Mound area in *Ancient Monuments of the Mississippi Valley*, by Squire and Davis.

At about the same time, word of the strange earthworks had reached beyond Adams County to Chillicothe, the former state capital about fifty miles distant that had its own enormous, mysterious earthworks complex. The editor of a Chillicothe weekly newspaper, the *Scioto Gazette*, regularly explored these earthworks, and when the American Ethnological Society called on him to create a systematic examination of the mounds, Ephraim George Squire joined with Chillicothe physician and amateur archaeologist Edwin Hamilton Davis in 1845. Together the pair explored what was then known as the western states, conducting careful surveys and analyses of thousands of mounds and earthworks. In 1848, Squire submitted a manuscript with meticulous etchings describing their findings to the American Ethnological Society, which sought the financial assistance of the brand-new Smithsonian Institution. The artfully produced and significant *Ancient Monuments of the Mississippi Valley* became the Smithsonian Institution's first book.

Among all their findings across the Midwest, the snake effigy on the plateau in Adams County dazzled Squire and Davis. "Probably the most extraordinary earthwork thus far discovered at the West is the Great Serpent," wrote Squire, who penned the book's language. "No plan or description has hitherto been published; nor does the fact of its existence appear to have been known beyond the secluded vicinity in which it occurs. The notice first received by the authors of these researches was exceedingly vague and indefinite."[12] Accompanied by an extraordinarily detailed etching, their verbal description of the earthwork painted a defined picture:

> *Conforming to the curve of the hill, and occupying its very summit, is the serpent, its head resting near the point, and its body winding back for seven hundred feet, in graceful undulations, terminating in a triple coil at the tail. The entire length, if extended, would be not less than one thousand feet....* [The work] *is clearly and boldly defined, the embankment being upwards of five feet in height by thirty feet base, at the centre of the body, but diminishing somewhat towards the head and tail. The neck of the serpent is stretched out and slightly curved, and its mouth is opened wide as if in the act of swallowing or ejecting an oval figure, which rests partially within the distended jaws.*[13]

Chapter 3

PUBLICITY

Ancient Monuments of the Mississippi Valley exposed the Adams County serpent far beyond local curiosity. "In 1848, [Serpent Mound] becomes world renowned," says local historian Delsey Wilson.[14] Its fame was confirmed when landowner James P. Lovett purchased more property around the hilltop and named his nearly four hundred acres Great Serpent Farm. But Lovett seems not to have appreciated the significance of the twisting, raised earth. Although the land was totally engulfed in forest when it was studied by Squire and Davis in 1846, in 1860 a tornado swept across the hilltop, erasing the forest that had shrouded the plateau and opening the land that included the effigy to Lovett's mule and plow for the next several planting seasons.

In 1864, the mound changed hands again when James P. Lovett died and the property became a gift for his heirs. In 1870, John J. Lovett consolidated ownership with the purchase of half the acreage from his brother David, but unlike his brothers, John recognized the importance of the earthworks and held them back from cultivation after he purchased the property from David. John almost immediately welcomed archaeologists, a new kind of explorers. The Reverend John Patterson MacLean, a Universalist minister of Hamilton, Ohio, and A.B. French became the first of these scientists when they visited the Great Serpent for a visual examination in June 1883. MacLean, accompanied by the Reverend Jacob Tener, returned in May the following year to survey the works, and on October 20, "by the direction of the Bureau of Ethnology," he continued his measurements with the assistance of T.E. Crider, superintendent of the Hamilton County, Ohio waterworks.

MacLean, already a respected archaeological researcher, reported that the land around the serpent had been cultivated after the 1860 tornado, "but the effigies bear no trace of having been disturbed by the plow." He observed that the undulations of the serpent rose slightly above the level of the plateau and that "the works…are so located as not to be seen until one is upon them," while the head of the serpent had almost disappeared. MacLean, unlike Squire and Davis, noted the addition of a mounded wall of about three feet in height in the shape of a leaping frog. A giant egg-shaped wall, about two feet in height and enclosing a damaged stone altar, lay between the legs of the frog. MacLean's careful measurements continued across the entire earthwork. "Leaving the neck [of the serpent] we find the body makes graceful curves and undulation," MacLean wrote, measuring a total distance from head to tail of slightly more than one thousand feet.[15]

Next to view the serpent was the respected Frederic W. Putnam, who was to become known as the "Father of Archaeology."[16] Putnam, director of Harvard College's Peabody Museum, fulfilled a desire to see the works described by Squire and Davis, MacLean and others when in September 1883 he took the seven-hour trip from Cincinnati by rail and wagon into the southern Ohio hills. Serpent Mound stunned him:

> *Reclining on the huge folds of this gigantic serpent, as the last rays of the sun dancing from the distant hilltops cast their long shadows over the valley, I mused on the probabilities of the past; and there seemed to come to me a picture of a distant time, of people with strange customs, and with it came the demand for an interpretation of this mystery. The unknown must become known!*[17]

Putnam said that although MacLean a few months before had reported otherwise, the undulations of the serpent appeared to have been plowed, but now redbud trees, sumac and weeds covered them. He immediately asked landowner John Lovett to clear the effigy of the underbrush, and a day later, with the entirety of the serpent now visible, Putnam was confirmed in his desire to preserve the unique structure.

"On my return to the East I took every opportunity of urging the importance of preserving the Serpent Mound," he wrote. "In 1885 I again visited the serpent, and finding that its destruction was inevitable unless immediate measures were taken for its preservation, I secured a contract that it should remain intact for a year."[18] Landowner John Lovett had in fact explored options to sell the property to farmers, whose patience would

Frederic Ward Putnam, by T. Smutney, 1900. *Courtesy Peabody Museum, Harvard University.*

Alice Fletcher, circa 1893. *From* Popular Science Monthly, *vol. 43.*

not be unending. At about the same time, another scientist promoted Putnam's efforts in Boston.

Alice Cunningham Fletcher had become known in scholarly circles as a self-taught expert on the Indigenous populations of America. She was supporting herself as a "noted lecturess" when she met Putnam around 1870 and her scholarly zeal impressed him, so at his invitation, she became an apprentice in archaeology at the Peabody Museum. While her interests lay mostly in the study of western Native American tribes (with whom she lived in the early 1880s), her studies led Fletcher to the issue of preserving the old monuments Squire and Davis had identified. The Cahokia earthworks in Illinois and Serpent Mound in Ohio especially caught her attention, so during an 1886 presentation at the home of classics scholar Ellen Mason in Newport, Rhode Island, she focused on Putnam's efforts to halt the potential loss of the serpent.

Fletcher's talk sparked the women to begin an organization for the preservation of antiquities, and Fletcher immediately alerted Putnam, noting, "They are all rich."[19] Putnam responded with a fact sheet that he forwarded to the women, who before the end of 1886 had collected just under $6,000 for purchase of the Serpent Mound property. This fund was signed over to the trustees of the Peabody Museum of Harvard, and in May 1887, Putnam returned to Adams County to redeem John Lovett's promise to sell the grounds. In the meantime, Lovett had sold all of Serpent Mound Farm to John T. Wilson for $8,160, and Wilson in turn sold a 58.7-acre portion of the property to the Trustees of the Peabody Museum for $6,000. Later that summer, Putnam was able to secure another 2.0 acres, and that summer he invited a crew of his archaeology students to join him. They immediately pitched tents and began a thorough, three-year systematic study of the earthworks.

Putnam introduced meticulous scientific anthropology into his procedures. He and his Harvard students first mapped the earthworks, finding the

raised area covered a straight-line distance of 496 feet and had a total length, following the undulations of the serpent, of 1,254 feet. The width of the mounded earth, as Putnam saw it, averaged about 20 feet; effects of weathering, plowing and, more recently, human intervention had lowered the mound to about 4 to 5 feet.[20]

To examine the substance of the earthwork and perhaps its purpose, Putnam and his colleagues dug seven trenches across its width, beginning at the mysterious oval "egg." The professor, then approaching fifty years old and described as a tall, powerfully built man with dark hair and whiskers,[21]

Putnam and crew at Serpent Mound. *Courtesy Peabody Museum, Harvard University.*

would stand with his notebook in one hand and an umbrella in the other, sheltering himself from the scorching sun's rays (which at times reached 103 degrees Fahrenheit) while guiding a half-dozen workers. The crew drove stakes into the earth to carefully identify the study area and then removed sod and troweled away soil "inch by inch," sifting and depositing it behind the digging crew.

Putnam at a dig. *Courtesy Peabody Museum, Harvard University.*

The caretakers of the Great Serpent Farm, the family of Daniel Wallace and his wife, Jenny Ferguson Wallace, lived in a log cabin on the property and assisted the research team. Several Wallace generations—including Daniel's brother Newton; his father, William; and his elderly grandfather Alexander—helped dig and provided a team of oxen to haul dirt. When the archaeology work was completed, the family built a small log museum to display artifacts that had been found.[22]

At the end of the summer of 1889, Putnam closed the excavations and personally set about restoring the earthworks to what he believed was their original appearance. Using the diagrams created by Squire and Davis and others who preceded him, as well as his own notes on the inner volume of the earthworks, he had the dirt shoveled back into place and then personally troweled the surfaces smooth. After the ground was prepared, bluegrass seed was spread over it, and a few native tree saplings were planted. Putnam envisioned a parklike setting that would advance recognition of the area as a shrine, so he and his crew built a path around the curves of the serpent to encourage orderly examination of it, and signs were posted to warn visitors to stay off the earthworks. Formerly cultivated areas nearby were reclaimed as meadows, and proper trails were constructed up from Brush Creek below to the summit of the hill. Putnam made plans to formally preserve the site. He wrote:

> *So long as the place is respected and guarded by all who visit it, the park will be free to all, but should any vandalism be committed, an arrangement would at once be made to put a keeper in place, and possibly entrance fees*

Top: Serpent Mound effigy grounds after renewal in 1889. *Courtesy Peabody Museum, Harvard University*.

Bottom: Serpent Mound effigy grounds after 1889 renewal with paths. *Courtesy Peabody Museum, Harvard University.*

> *would have to be charged in order to pay the expense. But certainly the people will respect a place thus gratuitously prepared and opened for their benefit, to see and enjoy, but not to injure.*[23]

At the same time, Putnam and Professor M.C. Reed of Hudson, Ohio, petitioned the Ohio state legislature for special recognition of the state's venerable earthworks. The legislature responded with an act passed in March 1888 stating that any earthwork "purchased by any person, association, or company for the purpose of the preservation of said earthwork, and are not held for profit, but are or shall be dedicated to public uses…shall be exempt from taxation."[24] This was the first such legislation in the country.

In 1900, Harvard's Peabody Museum deeded ownership of the property to the Ohio Archaeological and Historical Society, which retains ownership to this day. The Society maintained the property through the twentieth century as a tranquil reserve under Putnam's theory of "quiet contemplation," but a great increase in the number of tourists following the Great Depression of the 1930s forced change to a philosophy of recreation, with attendant issues of lack of respect for the property. Serpent Mound became something of a controversial site in the last quarter of the century, and the Ohio Historical

"Egg" of effigy with stone "altar" after renewal in 1889. *Courtesy Peabody Museum, Harvard University.*

Stone marker at Serpent Mound State Memorial with coils of the serpent's tail in background. *Author photo.*

Society designated the Arc of Appalachia Preserves system, a project of Highlands Sanctuary, Inc., as the managing agency of Serpent Mound from 2010 until March 2021. In March 2021, the Ohio Historical Society, now renamed the Ohio History Connection, took back active management of the site. In 1976, the National Park Service recognized the site as a National Historic Landmark, and as of 2024, UNESCO was considering Serpent Mound as a World Heritage cultural site.

So Serpent Mound Park rose out of obscurity to become a recognized archaeological site. It would not rest quietly, however; its origins, purpose and even Putnam's own restoration would become matters of controversy.

Chapter 4

WITH PUTNAM AT THE SERPENT MOUND CAMP

When F.W. Putnam splashed across Brush Creek in 1883 at the bottom of a one-hundred-foot cliff in Adams County, Ohio, he had no plans other than investigation of several earthworks in the southern Ohio area with four fellow archaeologists. The arduous trip that had taken them from Hillsboro, Ohio, by wagon was supposed to include the Fort Hill hilltop earthworks enclosure and other nearby works such as the Seip Mound complex on the banks of Paint Creek, but when Dr. Putnam climbed through the brush to the plateau above Brush Creek, the scene intrigued him with "the most singular sensation of awe and admiration."[25] Reclining against one of the folds of the serpent effigy, he was inspired to begin a decade-long process of investigation and preservation at the site.

Beginning in the summer of 1887, Putnam established a camp with several tents and began investigations by digging trenches in the serpent earthwork that identified its structure and the careful planning its creators had used to build it. To accompany him in his endeavors, each summer from 1887 to 1889 he invited up to nine assistants, including Harvard students, to join the work. He did not record the identity of these assistants, other than the name of Dr. Charles L. Metz, a Cincinnati physician friend of Dr. Putnam. However, a detailed handwritten report about the 1889 activities at Serpent Mound, possibly a seminar term paper, says six student assistants lived in the tents constructed on the site. Archaeologist and author William F. Romain, in a 1980s archaeology study within the greater archaeological research at Serpent Mound, speculates that Putnam established the camp

Putnam relaxing on the effigy slope. *Courtesy Peabody Museum, Harvard University.*

Serpent Mound camp tent with occupant, possibly Dr. Charles L. Metz. *Courtesy Peabody Museum, Harvard University.*

about two hundred yards south of the serpent effigy, near the edge of the bluff overlooking the Brush Creek valley.[26]

In addition to Putnam and Metz, there are hints that of six students who accompanied Putnam in 1889, two were female. A photo taken at the site shows Putnam, Metz, three men and two women, and the paper by the anonymous author lists a woman paleontologist who "had a taste for fossils and went about, hammer in hand, seeking small shells with long names, looking wise but feeling hopelessly lost in the new region in which she found herself." Another student had an interest in botany, and another was an ornithologist fascinated by the birds of the area.[27] If a woman wrote the report, that would round out the crew of six young scholars.

This would be in tune with Dr. Putnam's lifelong efforts to recruit women as archaeologists. Putnam's cooperation with Alice Fletcher was, of course, instrumental in the acquisition and preservation of Serpent Mound Park, and he worked with women "involved in the more 'acceptable' support roles of the Victorian period, as well as women 'breaking the mold' doing independent research," explains St. Louis anthropology professor David L. Bowman.[28] Putnam taught anthropology courses at Radcliffe College, the women's institution affiliated with Harvard, as early as 1880 and persuaded colleagues to teach parallel anthropology classes to female students taking Harvard classes that were at the time segregated by sex.

Top: Serpent Mound camp scene with women third from left and far right. *Courtesy Peabody Museum, Harvard University.*

Bottom: Serpent Mound in 1889, showing camp tents with a female occupant. *Courtesy Peabody Museum, Harvard University*.

The unnamed author of the 1889 term paper described the goal of the student group accompanying Putnam at Serpent Mound as seeking "in a dilettante way, the genuine everyday life of the original denizens of this lovely region."[29] The archaeologists found much evidence of human habitation, as remains of bones of deer, elk, bear, turtles, fish and birds "told us of the former abundance of animals, many of which are now extinct in this region." The group was fascinated by the constant supply of found artifacts: broken pots, flint knives, hammers, scrapers and ornaments carved in stone, so that the summer's research allowed them to contemplate the lifestyle of the "original denizens."

One incident allowed the group to pretend more vividly that they were engaged in a long bygone way of life. According to the anonymous author of the report, the group enjoyed cooked meals, enabled after the men of the camp had dug a trench, laid wooden fence rails in it and bordered it with slabs of limestone so that it could hold hot coals. Over these they placed rods of iron to hold pots and pans. But one evening, the contraption collapsed and "our dinner was lost in the ashes, though fortunately our implements, being made of iron rather than earthenware, withstood the test…and did not break."[30] Otherwise the group ate well, with breakfast, "moveable lunches" and dinner served at 6:30 p.m. each day. Evenings were spent around a campfire, reviewing the day's activities or listening to discussions about natural history, after which, sleepy after a long day in the open air, they would "wander to [their] tents under the brilliant light of the stars" to be lulled to sleep by the monotonous hum of the katydid, "the mournful 'who, who, who' of the owls while the whippoorwill and the screech owl would give variety to the chorus."[31]

Probably the members of the 1889 research group lived a life somewhat more comfortable than that of the prehistoric Native Americans who preceded them there. The anonymous author described their settlement as seven tents and a nearby covered cooking area, located under oak trees and out of sight of curious tourists. Their tents, made of double layers of canvas, were secure but unbearable in the afternoon heat, which at times surpassed one hundred degrees Fahrenheit. However, the campers enjoyed cool breezes wafting up from the creek, and the tents had wood plank floors. "With cot beds we were not martyrs in our camp life," the anonymous author wrote, adding that "the freedom of the life was perfectly delightful and refreshing."[32] The report includes numerous references to the natural beauty of the area, with varied forest growth of chestnut, sycamore, buckeye and black walnut trees.

Sometimes the natural environment interrupted their slumber. On more than one occasion, some member of the group would rise and voice general alarm that brought out the campers, only to discover that the source of the disquiet was a dog or cat rummaging through dinner leftovers. The civilized eastern students nevertheless found such outdoor adventure exhilarating. "Fancy being able to slip on a dressing gown and shoes and go out in the

Interior of a typical Serpent Mound camp tent. *Courtesy Peabody Museum, Harvard University.*

early morning sunshine to get a glass of milk, sure of being as secluded as in your own house," the anonymous author wrote.[33]

The camp employed a full-time cook who prepared "peculiar" meals and learned some "simple dishes" from the easterners on hand. The camp had its own cow, so with fresh milk, native apples and berries they "fared well and were content." The cook, a young lady of the neighborhood, stared at the archaeologists with unblinking "little coal-black eyes, but the thoughts that were behind them were past our finding out. She probably judged us to be harmless lunatics, but as she was paid very liberally, earning as much during our stay as during the whole year besides, she bore with our vagaries," recalled the anonymous author.[34]

Interaction with the cook illustrated vast cultural differences. If she was offered something she didn't want, "she invariably said 'I would not wish it,'" the writer observed. The young cook did not offer precise directions to her home, merely indicating her address was "quite a piece away, right over yonder and up that-a-way," but the anonymous author of the report probably would not have voluntarily traveled to the cook's home. Roads,

Serpent Mound camp cooking area with the group's cow, held by a woman, probably the camp's cook. A second woman stands to the right. *Courtesy Peabody Museum, Harvard University.*

which the residents of the rural area called "pikes," had only recently formed connections among the isolated communities, and "the old dirt roads are terrible—in dry times they are deeply gullied and after a rain they become veritable sloughs of despair," the anonymous author said. They were made all the more scornful by the uncomfortable nine-mile wagon ride the students had to endure from the train station in Peebles to the Serpent Mound Park. Nor did the small local communities of the area offer any attraction. "It is a cheerless, tasteless, undesirable place," said the writer, who viewed the archaeological work of the Harvard crew as "a great civilizer and educator: In the first place nothing is of any value in this part of Ohio unless it has to do directly or indirectly with pork, and a 'right smart bunch of hogs' is the chief aim of life."[35]

In return, inhabitants of the area were puzzled by the painstaking archaeological digging with its associated detail work. Yet visitors arrived in droves: despite its obscure location, accessible only by poor roads, in the summer of 1889 alone about three thousand tourists came to the site from as far away as Alaska and as close as an hour's buggy ride away.[36] Many of them found it difficult to understand what the researchers were doing, as the concept of tiresome excavation for no monetary gain seemed beyond them. Some believed the crew to be in the oil business, while others suggested the earthworks would yield buried treasures. In one incident recounted in the term paper, an older man "who had studied and who had an air of superiority" drew particular attention by his attempt to debate with Putnam:

> *"We've been to the serpent and we want to talk over the mystery of it* [the man said]. *You call that a natural formation, do you?" No, the professor replied. It was carefully planned, laid out and made by the people who inhabited these villages. "Yes," said the stranger, "I thought so. Well, you call that a worshipful mound, do you?" Professor Putnam responded that in his opinion it was a shrine dedicated to the worship of the serpent.... The professor, now fairly interested, launched into a full account of the serpent in particular and all other mounds in general and with a comparison of various earthworks to be found in the country.*[37]

Such erudition fascinated the Harvard students, who were in awe of Dr. Putnam. They observed that for the professor, "everything is in dead earnest, from the study of the tiniest chigger with his inseparable friend, his pocket lens, to the preservation of the Serpent mound."[38] Putnam was seen working from morning to dusk, standing in the trenches with trowel in hand, from the beginning with his first on-site camp in 1887, when he and the men of his crew dug initial trenches into the Serpent Mound effigy itself, to later excavations in mounds a few hundred yards south of the serpent. His method was "a marvel of thoroughness," the report writer said.[39]

With his orderly procedures, Putnam found that the mound's builders had put a great deal of thought into planning the effigy. When the researchers dug seven trenches and exposed the outside edge of the serpent effigy, Putnam personally used a trowel to continue to clear the edge of the serpentine mound[40] and found that its shape had been defined with clay and ash. (Later studies suggested that the serpent shape had been defined by a thin line of stones sealed together with clay.)[41] In his own comprehensive report of the Serpent Mound project, published in 1890, he wrote that to create the body of the earthwork, topsoil had been removed and a foot-deep layer of yellow clay deposited, followed by "dark soil" or "vegetable mould.... In some places, particularly at the western end of the oval, and where the serpent approached the steeper portions of the hill, the base layer was made with stones, as if to prevent its being washed away by heavy rains."[42] Nearby there were three depressions in the earth, which Putnam determined to be "borrow pits" from which earth had been removed in order to make the serpent. (Recent research has shown these to be mere natural sinkholes.)

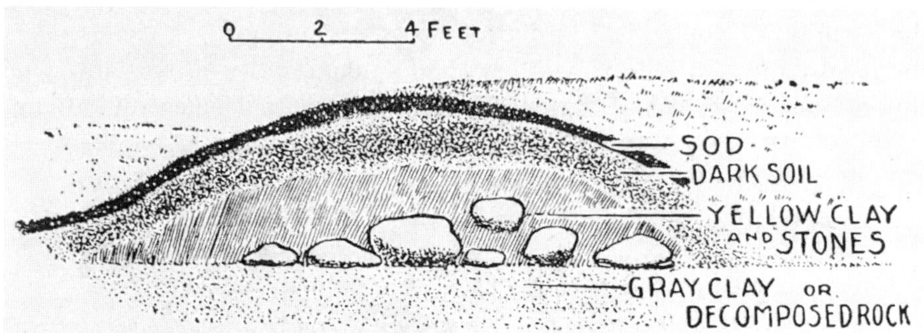

Cross-section of the Serpent Mound coil, showing construction layers. *From* Century Magazine *(1889–90), vol. 39.*

The researchers found no ornaments, tools or human remains in the serpent effigy. However, during digging in the area a few hundred yards south of the effigy, Putnam and his crews scratched up many small artifacts including flint chips, chisels, simple hammer-shaped stones, knives, pieces of pottery and ornaments. These led Putnam a couple hundred feet south, away from the serpent effigy, to the area along a winding gravel path that led from the county road up through the property. The professor had heard that this site originally rose a few feet above the surrounding area, but it had been plowed down. He observed the soil there was darker in color than the surrounding terrain, and wood stakes were driven to delineate the research area. Then "the clay below, for a foot in depth, was examined inch by inch, as the men worked forward in a line, throwing the earth behind them."[43] Their work exposed thousands of artifacts scattered on or near the surface, including "implements of various kinds," knives, drills and pottery. Burned spots, ash pits and the bones of fish, birds and mammals used as food indicated there had been fireplaces and dwellings.

The area also included many human burials. Following nineteenth-century archaeology practices that he pioneered, Putnam carefully exposed several burial sites at ground level by digging into them, although the contents already had been partially unearthed by plowing. Then the five-member crew moved to a small conical mound that also had been reduced in size by the plow, and when they systematically dissected it with a trench, they found an interment. Farther on, Putnam and the students explored a somewhat larger conical mound with several intrusive graves dug into the side of the mound, indicating that more recent peoples had recognized the location as sacred and continued its funereal use. Putnam's investigators next moved to a nearby oblong mound where digging exposed the remains of nine individuals, the oldest (lowest in the mound structure) being a man buried with great ceremony, as indicated by numerous artifacts including axe heads, arrow points and a copper plate. Above this interment, earth had been raised to form a mound of about twelve feet height, and eight later burials had been inserted into its sides, some shallow enough that recent cultivation had exposed tools and artifacts. Adjoining this site to the east and south, Putnam's crew unearthed two more graves that Putnam judged to be older because they contained nothing other than the human remains.

Results of excavation of some mounds suggested for the professor several methods of ancient funeral ceremonies. In one spot, it appeared that the skeletal remains of three humans had been transported to the site; in a larger mound, an area of seventy feet in diameter had been stripped of earth and clay and a clay platform placed in it. On this, a fire was kindled and burned for some time, as indicated by the remains of large logs. Then on these ashes was placed the body of a young, six-foot-tall man, after which earth and clay were mounded over the body to a height of about twelve feet. In subsequent years, after the earth had settled, this mound was the site of intrusive burials. In all the locations around this site, implements including flint knives, arrowheads and stone tools had been buried. One other mound in particular yielded many fine artifacts, described by Putnam as "the largest number of objects I have ever seen in a single grave," and the burial of two people. However, despite careful searching, the archaeologists could not locate the skulls of these individuals, leading Putnam to surmise that these were the ceremonial places of renowned heroes, victims of warfare whose lives were celebrated with the burial.

Overall, the excavations revealed that the area had been something of a cemetery that had been used over many years, with burials and apparent cremations made both before and after the serpent effigy was raised. In total, Putnam and his students opened about twenty-three human graves. Following accepted archaeology of the time, they carefully unearthed the remains, photographed them and then catalogued and packed the items "so that the process of investigating a mound may be quite satisfactorily done in Cambridge by studying the photographs and comparing that to the specimens found," one member of the crew explained.[44]

By the close of his summer session in 1889, Professor Putnam was able to form some conclusions and at the same time pose new questions. The Serpent Mound site had never been much of a human settlement, he determined, but it was a "sacred shrine [where] ceremonies of great importance had taken place."[45] On the other hand, his research and all the

Serpent Mound effigy after renewal in 1888. *Courtesy Peabody Museum, Harvard University.*

excavation could not answer "with pick and shovel" the basic question of purpose: "Here before me was the mysterious work of an unknown people, whose seemingly most sacred place we had invaded. Was this a symbol of an old serpent faith, here on the western continent, which from the earliest time in the religions of the East held many people enthralled?"[46] In this statement, he hinted at his belief that the serpent motif had been brought forth from the great cultures of the Yucatán and Mesoamerica, a theory that he passed on to the student author of the term paper who recorded the research. "This combination of natural features probably could not be found again in any part of the great route along which the people must have journeyed from Mexican sites. Is all this to be taken as mere coincidence in the development of a faith in America and in the Old World?" the writer asked.[47]

Putnam, in his original description of the property, stated that he wanted to restore the grounds to their appearance as seen by Squire and Davis in 1845. He wrote that he had been motivated by the impending loss of the earthworks, laid bare by a tornado and then scraped by precipitation and plows. After he secured ownership and carefully incised the site himself for research purposes over three summers, the professor initiated a thorough restoration and improvement process. "It is difficult to realize the great labor which Professor Putnam has devoted to the task of restoration," the

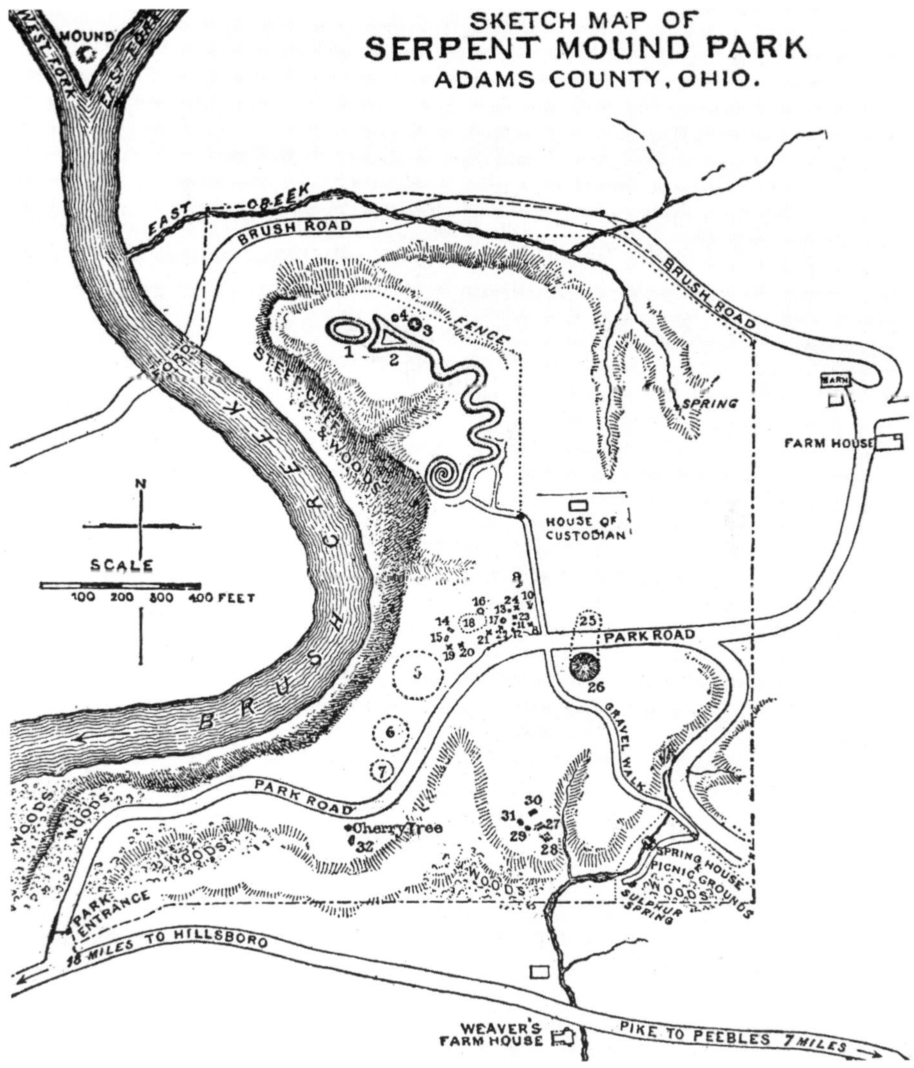

Serpent Mound Park sketched in 1890 by F.W. Putnam, showing mounds and artifact sites. Numbers indicate dig sites. *From* Century Illustrated Monthly Magazine, *vol. 89*.

student writer observed. "Professor Putnam would not trust the work of repair to anyone but himself, and he worked from early morning till dusk for many long days, trowel in hand."[48] Putnam had dirt that was removed from the trenches returned to its original location, and then he smoothed the surface and sowed bluegrass seed so the surface would not erode. The researchers then planted dozens of native trees around the area, fenced it and added a gate. Horses, not permitted on the grounds, got their own hitching posts and watering trough at the bottom of the hill, at the entrance to the park from the pike. A sign proclaimed the new Serpent Mound Park and the fact that it would remain free of charge to visitors.

With the work completed, Putnam and his crew departed the new park with great reluctance. "What did it all amount to?" the term paper author asked the professor. "What have you found to recompense you for such an expenditure of muscle in each dry-as-dust exploration as this has proved to be?" The response was that "these mounds are as instructive in their way as those that are filled with treasure."[49] Ultimately, the Great Serpent enthralled both the students and the professor in almost identical ways. The student chronicler mused about life under the full moon of midsummer and observed:

> *You are sure to be alone and free from visitors and can yield unrestrainedly to the beauty of the time and place, and allow your mind to come under the full sway of the imagination. It would not require much of an effort to make you fancy that the hills were thronging with a busy multitude in whose presence you have intruded, an unwelcome guest.*[50]

Professor Putnam, who was captivated from the moment in 1883 when he first reclined on one of the coils of the effigy, wrote that the mound had a "strange, lifelike appearance." He wrote:

> *Late in the afternoon, when the lights and shades are brought out in strong relief, the effect is indeed strange and weird; and the effect is heightened still more when the full moon lights up the scene.... That such a work, so carefully designed and constructed under such difficulties along this narrow ridge terminating in the high rough cliff, was planned and built under some powerful influence, we can but believe.*[51]

Chapter 5

RESTORATION?

Raccoons delighted Serpent Mound Park visitors at the turn of the twentieth century. The trusted Daniel Wallace was installed by Professor Putnam as custodian of Serpent Mound Park when Putnam wrapped up site research in 1889, and Wallace, who had lived as a tenant of the Lovetts in the farmhouse on the property, kept a pair of pet raccoons that he walked on leashes around the grounds.[52] Wallace and his family had helped Putnam in his excavation work, and he was recognized as the local authority on the earthwork, "a most competent and faithful official."[53] He held paid positions as caretaker from the time of Putnam's work until his death in 1916.

The museum had spent thousands of dollars bringing the property up to proper standards for tourists, but its distance from the Boston area made it a remote artifact. Serpent Mound Park needed constant attention: park roads established by Putnam were washing out, and a neighbor's hogs rooted through the park's mounds, causing considerable damage. Deterioration came to the attention of E.O. Randall, general secretary of the Ohio State Archaeological and Historical Society (OSAHS), who contacted Putnam in 1894 and suggested the Ohio group could better protect the grounds. The trustees of Harvard College agreed, and in 1900, they voted to transfer ownership of the Serpent Mound Park, for the sum of one dollar, to the OSAHS.[54] Terms of the transfer stipulated that the "grantee Society shall provide for the perpetual care of the Serpent Mound, and for keeping the

Serpent Mound Park as a free public park forever."[55] Further, the society was to create a "suitable" plaque or monument recognizing the transfer and conditions of ownership.

Thus, after 1900, Wallace's employer became the Ohio State Archaeological and Historical Society, with Wallace reporting directly to Randall, who rarely visited the site. The custodian put his initial attention to drainage and then around 1904 to construction of a kitchen and outbuildings for the farmhouse. At the same time, the society began to advertise its holdings widely, including photos and drawings it displayed at the 1904 World's Fair in St. Louis. With the public's greater knowledge of the site, the society found that it needed to accommodate the resulting tourists. In order to provide a near-complete view of the earthwork, a steel observation tower was built on the grounds in 1908 by Columbus Steel and Wire for $500,[56] and by the fall of 1919, the society's Committee on Serpent Mound Park reported that a shelter house including a museum had been built. The custodian, now Guy Wallace, son of Daniel, reported 6,200 visitors had registered at the park in the past year.[57]

In 1929, the OSAHS constructed a picnic shelter in the park, a signal that the society had shifted the governing philosophy of Serpent Mound State Memorial from the "quiet contemplation" envisioned by Putnam to recreation for the masses, as exemplified by the annual Adams County Reunions on the grounds that attracted as many as ten thousand people beginning in 1929. Automobiles were rolling to the site on improved local roads, so their motorists had to have a place to park; visitors needed improved restroom facilities; and proper drainage continued to be an issue. According to comprehensive research by architectural historian Rory Krupp,[58] these needs came at a critical time for park officials because the Great Depression stripped away funding for Ohio state appropriations. At the same time, national unemployment rolls greatly expanded[59] (U.S. unemployment increased by 20 percent between 1929 and 1933) and the U.S. government, to put people to work, founded agencies such as the Civil Works Administration (CWA), the Federal Emergency Relief Administration (FERA) and the Civilian Conservation Corps (CCC). These agencies had a significant effect on Serpent Mound property.

Crews of the CWA began to modify the park in 1933 when they started to build restroom facilities, created with bricks from the dismantled 1823 Second Baptist Church in Clarksville, Ohio. According to Krupp, that project was completed by FERA workers, older transients who had drifted into Ohio from adjacent states following rumors of better relief pay. These

Adams County Reunion, circa 1940, at Serpent Mound State Memorial. *Private collection.*

FERA workers set up a camp on the Serpent Mound grounds and completed the restroom building in 1934.

The OSAHS had begun work at Serpent Mound Park with a lengthy application list including restoration of the effigy. Although Henry R. McPherson, the society's curator of state memorials, and Erwin Zepp, the society's landscape architect, attempted to oversee modifications of the grounds, the assortment of agencies and varying personnel groups at work, with differing skill levels and equipment, made that supervision difficult. Krupp reports that although the first CWA groups were limited to picks and shovels, later and supposedly more skilled FERA and WPA crews used heavy equipment, including dynamite, to remove old buildings and driveways and build parking lots. Federal money totaling $200,000 funded WPA crews who worked on the property and constructed a new superintendent's residence and service building.[60] Then CCC crews—young people ages eighteen to twenty-five—set up camp at nearby Fort Hill State Memorial and came to Serpent Mound Park to focus on drainage projects and cleanup.

Works Projects Administration (WPA) workers in 1937 constructed this lookout and steps leading from the Serpent to the Gorge Trail in the valley below the effigy. *National Archives WPA Information Division Photographs, Negative 12259.*

The philosophy that governed all the work attempted to restore the park to its supposed original state. Explains Krupp, "The buildings and landscape at Serpent Mound State Memorial were changed after 1936 to reflect National Park Service village design precepts, transitioning from an American bourgeois leisure landscape to a village design with naturalistic landscaping."[61] That meant haphazardly restoring the height of the effigy and mounds of the park, probably with fill from the parking lot and restroom construction and certainly without the direction of on-site archaeologists.

The revised dimensions of the serpent effigy remained undisturbed until the 1970s, when the research team of Clark Hardman and Marjorie Hardman determined that the effigy had never been mapped accurately. Noting that they were "mildly exasperated" by traditional maps of the earthwork and the effects of 1930s restoration,[62] they found that Putnam, in his studies of the earthworks, used drawings by Squire and Davis and MacLean that varied by as much as ten feet. In June 1979, they used surveying equipment

Depression-era restroom building at Serpent Mound State Memorial. *Author photo.*

and a 1960 aerial photograph to visually re-create portions of the serpent's head and undulations and fixed a basic unit of measure as the long length of the "egg" shape at the mouth of the serpent. They guessed that the earthen oval was the first element of the effigy constructed[63] and applied its measure and then its short width—exactly half of the length—to evaluate the size and width of the snake's undulations. They said that the direction of these curves was found to indicate summer and winter solstices at the site. "The relationships [we] pointed out…suggest the Great Serpent people had a knowledge of the apparent movement of the sun along the horizon and some knowledge of geometry and arithmetic including linear measures," the Hardmans wrote.[64]

Archaeologist William Romain followed by suggesting several environmental factors influenced the effigy's location.[65] In a 1988 report, he saw it was placed on the edge of a five-mile-wide crater—the origin of which was not yet determined—that caused uplifted rocks and magnetic disturbances. In addition, he observed that the area of the effigy is located within an environment of high uranium ore concentration, as well as oil and acidic groundwater that seeps from its limestone bedrock. According to Romain, underground water dissolved surface features and created sinkholes near the effigy that were originally thought to be borrow pits. In the 1970s, one of these pits collapsed, exposing a crevice about eight feet deep that the Mound Park management had to fill with gravel.

Romain and other researchers also criticized the accuracy of the Hardmans' mapping, and work on measurement of the effigy continued. The team of Robert Fletcher and Terry Cameron complained in 1986 that "none of the previous maps or drawings in the existing literature were particularly accurate"[66] and commissioned their own aerial photography. Independently, a group of Wright State University students and faculty in September 1987 set up on the effigy a series of survey stations that coincided with measurements by Fletcher and Cameron and then conducted a ground-penetrating radar survey of the site. These projects confirmed that the effigy's builders had carefully planned and laid out their work. "The elegance of the design is even more remarkable considering the size of the mound," Fletcher and Cameron said.[67] However, the researchers were forced to admit their observations were based on earthworks that had been modified in the 1930s, and thus they questioned the authenticity and age of the constructions.

This query led researchers to renew their digging. In the early 1990s, a research team of Midwest archaeologists requested permission from the Ohio Historical Society (successor to the Ohio State Archaeological and Historical Society) to start poking holes in the park earthworks, and these generated controversial results. In July 1991, they drilled core samples in areas of the serpent where the earth appeared to have settled, suggesting sites where Putnam had dug trenches into the effigy during his 1887–89 research. These cores did indeed indicate the locations of Putnam trenches, which were reopened and studied. The digs mostly confirmed Putnam's conclusions, with the additional observation that Putnam had underestimated the effects of plowing on the original surface of the effigy. More importantly, the researchers sifted out 158 flint chips, which the researchers determined to have come from Ohio's Flint Ridge (an ancient source of quality flint); 29 ceramic bits determined to have originated with prehistoric potters; and fragments of wood and bone.[68]

Putnam had determined that a village dating to cultures that in his time were called Adena and Hopewell people had existed within a few hundred yards of the serpent effigy, a conclusion confirmed by the 1991 researchers. However, the 1991 group decided materials must have been transported to Serpent Mound in the 1930s "restorations," because Putnam had not found any artifacts in the serpent during his digging in the 1880s. Analysis of the organic materials gave more precise measurements: radiocarbon dating of an oak charcoal piece drawn from deep within the mound, far below the more modern backfill, indicated the wood dated from about AD 1000 to 1140.[69]

In 2017, the Ohio Historical Society, now renamed the Ohio History Connection (OHC), began further excavations to fix CCC work of the 1930s that had left artifacts clearly not original to Serpent Mound. The Depression-era workers had fashioned a set of stone steps over the mound near its tail, and to return Serpent Mound closer to its original form, the OHC sent a team to remove the stones, with archaeologists observing. The digging not only cleared the stone steps and revealed two large foundation blocks but also exposed previously unseen layers of dirt in the serpent. Taking this opportunity, a team led by OHC archaeology manager Bradley Lepper sifted through the soil that had been dug out and found a rivet from

Approximate site of a prehistoric Native American village, with a small mound to the right and the effigy earthwork in the distance to the left. *Author photo.*

blue jeans and several flakes of flint. They also dug and removed a small dirt sample about a foot deep at the bottom of the new trench and had it analyzed; carbon dating of oak charcoal fragments indicated the sample was buried about AD 1300.[70] The sandstone foundation blocks were left in place and the trench re-filled, thus returning Serpent Mound to its presumed more original appearance.

Chapter 6

WHAT IS IT?

Squire and Davis, who were among the first Caucasians to encounter Serpent Mound, wrote, "The true character of the work was apparent on the first inspection." The effigy is without question a snake, one about one thousand feet long, with four undulations and a curled tail. Squire and Davis estimated its height above the surrounding flat area as about five feet at the tallest, with a width at its base of about thirty feet, but by the time of Putnam's investigations, forces of nature and the plow had reduced the serpent to an earth mound raised about two to three feet above the surrounding ground. The area thought to be the head of the snake features two huge "jaws" that open around an egg-shaped earthen enclosure that had the burned remains of a stone altar at its center. Squire and David also noted two "horns" slightly less prominent above ground that protruded out from the head of the serpent; these were alternately recorded or omitted by later observers.

Professor Charles C. Willoughby of Harvard's Peabody Museum, which had purchased the property from farmers at Putnam's urging, visited the site in 1919 for careful measurement. He decided Squire and Davis had performed only a cursory review that Putnam mistakenly followed, and Willoughby observed further constructions between the egg and the edge of the outcropping, which he guessed to be the remains of a possibly forked tongue. Likewise, he emphasized a failure to restore the embankments at the base of the head, which he called horns typical of serpent images honored by Indigenous peoples.[71]

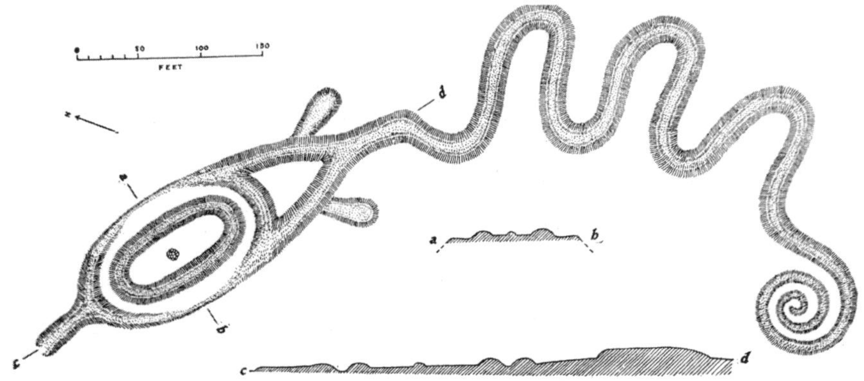

Fig. 15.—Plan and cross-sections of Serpent Mound, Adams Co., Ohio. C. C. Willoughby, 1918.

Serpent Mound drawing according to Willoughby, 1918. *From* American Anthropologist *21, no. 2 (April–June 1919).*

Native cultures have honored snakes for millennia. Researchers Webb and Snow suggest very early societies in what became the American Midwest worshiped the "Horned Serpent,"[72] and ethnologist Barbara Mann says Indigenous peoples traditionally recognized and respected the Great Horned Serpent. She suggests the oval portion of the Serpent Mound effigy, generally thought to represent an egg, instead depicts a "medicine bag," a bundle with powerful contents that empowered the Great Horned Serpent. The serpent in turn represented the dark regions below the earth, as opposed to the circle shape of many Midwest mounds, representing the sky.[73]

Mann also supports the theory that the serpent served as an observatory. The Hardmans and Fletcher and Cameron, in later studies, also offer less robust support for the snake as a winter solstice sunrise indicator but conclude the evidence suggests a "relatively intense preoccupation with the sun and solar phenomena."[74] Another suggestion is that the effigy depicts a bas-relief of a monster serpent, in profile on the flat tabletop of the promontory, swallowing the sun, a tilted flat circle, and causing an eclipse.[75] This theory would establish Serpent Mound as an important social center akin to our popular modern monuments in Washington, D.C.

Confusion continues as to the purpose of Serpent Mound largely because, as author Emerson Greenman noted, an accurate outline of the effigy is yet to be nailed down. "That Serpent Mound symbolized to the builders some religious or magical principle there can be no doubt," he said. "...Whether the serpent represented by this mound was a good or evil being will remain unknown." He added that to truly understand the purpose of the mound, it would be important to continue study of Indigenous people's relationship to serpents and to determine the Great Serpent Mound's original shape.[76]

What is "original" continues to be debated. From the time of Squire and Davis until today, there have been maps of the effigy including appendages that seem to come and go. The lithograph by the New York firm of Sarony and Major from the Squire and Davis sketch in 1846 illustrated only the effigy serpent and "egg-shaped" mound, with tiny raised areas at the neck of the serpent. Putnam, arguably the mound history's most thorough researcher, followed their plan. In 1885, MacLean added an entirely new effigy figure between the "egg" and the edge of the cliff above Brush Creek, an oval with what appeared to be legs extending toward the "egg" and two small arms. W.H. Holmes in 1886 suggested a wishbone-shaped earthwork crafted from the "legs" of MacLean's creature. Harvard's Willoughby kept the wishbone-shaped addition and added emphasis to the "ears" or "wings" attached to the neck of the serpent. Relatively recently, a multidisciplinary project by the team of Herrmann, et al. even announced evidence of a lost or discarded coil.[77]

These observations have led to a new theory of the effigy's purpose. Bradley Lepper, chief archaeologist of the Ohio History Connection, has proposed that the Serpent Mound effigy actually represents three

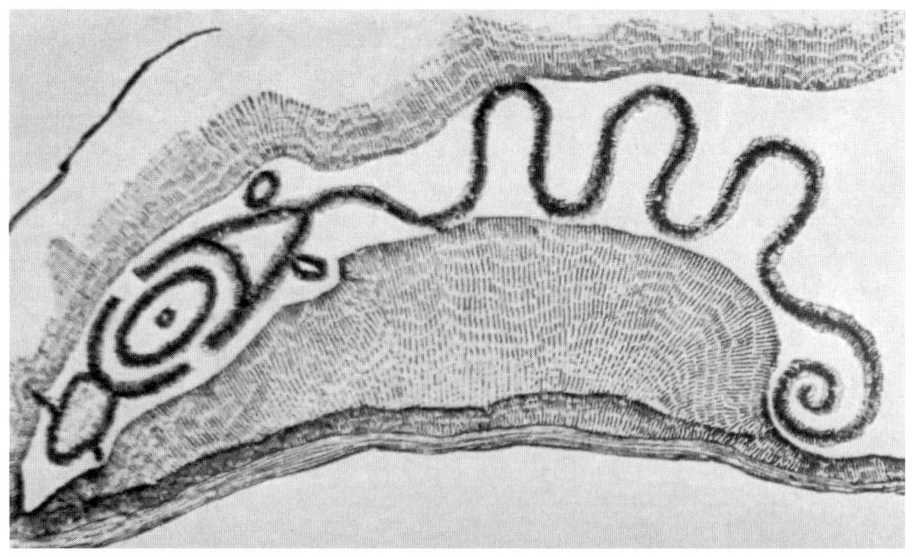

Serpent Mound drawing according to MacLean, 1885. *From* The Serpent Mound, Adams County, Ohio: Mystery of the Mound and History of the Serpent, *2nd ed., 1907.*

things: a four-legged creature with legs spread; the giant open oval; and the sinuous serpent, suggesting a fertility symbol and procreation. He and other researchers studied rock art in a Missouri cave, thought to have been created by Mississippian-era ancestors of the Dhegihan Sioux. The rock art included numerous images of serpents, to the extent that Lepper compared the elements and interactions in its many pictures to a Rosetta Stone that could help interpretation of the iconography of Serpent Mound.[78]

According to stories told by the Dhegihan Sioux, their ancestors migrated east from the Cahokia area. Analysis of climate patterns in the Mississippi Valley suggest that severe drought there between AD 1100 and 1250 influenced the people of mound cultures to move to the Ohio Valley. Those people brought with them myths of the Great Serpent and First Woman, which they depicted in the earthwork of the Serpent Mound, as well as other stories including the "underwater panther" depicted by the animal effigy at the nearby Alligator Mound in what is now Granville, Ohio.[79]

Lepper and geomorphologist Todd Frolking had taken advantage of an accidental deconstruction of the Alligator Mound effigy earthwork to study its construction and age. Located on a bluff above the same valley that passes the extensive Newark Earthworks in Newark, Ohio, the alligator structure takes the rough shape of a four-legged, tailed creature that appeared to be an alligator only in the eyes of early western explorers. One of its legs had been truncated in a construction accident, so Lepper in 1994 obtained permission from the Licking County Historical Society to investigate the scene. He found that the effigy had been constructed of stone and nearby earth, as earlier observers had noted, and he was able to collect a few small pieces of charcoal that he sent out for carbon dating. Results indicted the charcoal came from the period between AD 1170 to 1270, while the organic component of the soil in the effigy dated to around AD 1060. "All of the dates collectively argue strongly in support of a Late Prehistoric age for Alligator Mound" (in other words, around the time of the Fort Ancient Culture), the researchers conclude.[80]

Lepper suggested the earthwork was an outlier of the culture that created the many effigy earthworks of the upper Midwest. The four-legged motif illustrates an important creature of Native American tradition, the "Underwater Panther," which, with the Great Horned Serpent, ruled the underworld in opposition to the Thunderbird of the upper realm. Thus, the thinking goes, the same people who fled drought conditions of the upper Midwest for the verdant lands of the Ohio River Valley discovered plateaus overlooking what became known as Brush Creek and a similar location above what became the Licking River about 120 miles to the northeast. At these sites, they raised earthworks celebrating two major elements of their mythology. Suggests Lepper, "The effigy mounds, in their construction and use as shrines to the lords of the Underworld, would have been powerful unifying symbols for communities and regions"[81] that had transported their culture from previous centers in what is now the Upper Great Lakes area.

Ethnologist Barbara Mann calls Lepper's Underwater Panther "plausible," but she prefers to think of the Alligator Mound as a possum. The Underwater Panther belonged to groups west of the Mississippi River, she says, and although she maintains that Native American tradition supports the concept of pairs in everything natural, the linking of the Alligator Mound effigy with Serpent Mound as one-thousand-year-old constructions is, according to Mann, highly unlikely. She instead doubles that age: Serpent Mound represents a highly recognized cultural motif, the Horned Serpent, of about two thousand years ago,[82] and in a more recent publication, she cites Indigenous oral tradition that dates the Serpent Mound to four thousand years ago.[83]

Chapter 7

WHO?

Most European explorers who encountered the elaborate earthen mounds, walls and shapes of North America didn't know what to think of them. The origins of the works mystified the newcomers because the cultures Europeans met in the New World didn't fit the engineering standards of the Europeans. Indeed, there was serious dispute as to whether the Indigenous inhabitants around them were even people. Pope Paul III declared in 1537 that they were, and so they deserved to be converted, but even that promotion failed to convince white people that the Natives could have raised the mounds. Said author James Fergusson, in his 1872 volume on mounds in Europe and America:

> *The study of the manners and customs of the Red-man, who occupied North America when we first came in contact with them, is not at all likely to throw any light on the subject. They have never risen beyond the condition of hunters, and have no settled places of abode, and possess no works of art. The Mound Builders, on the contrary, were a settled people, certainly pastoral, probably to some extent even agricultural; they had fixed well chosen, unfortified abodes, altogether exhibiting a higher state of civilization than we have any reason to suppose the present race of Red-men ever reached or are capable of reaching.*[84]

Ethnologist Barbara Mann calls this theory "savagism."[85] Accordingly, the Indigenous peoples were considered brutes incapable of culture, so the mounds must have been produced by some long-lost advanced civilization. For example, Dr. Stephen Peet, editor of *American Antiquarian*, wrote at the birth of the twentieth century, "Mound builders were in a transition state between conditions of savagery and barbarism and that they had reached the point where animal worship is very prevalent."[86] Adams County history publisher J.A. Caldwell in 1880 described the Indigenous occupants of the area as "savages,"[87] and E.A. Allen, in an 1885 edition of the *American Antiquarian and Oriental Journal*, was "skeptical" of the level of civilization of the people supposed to have raised the earthworks.[88] He could scarcely believe that a people like the Native Americans could produce such complex works.

However, a few of the first white people to encounter the earthworks didn't entertain the "savages" theory. In 1632, Dominican missionary Gabriel Sagard watched as his Iroquois hosts built a mound.[89] Antoine-Simon Le Page du Pratz, a French writer living among the Natchez people in what would become Mississippi, recorded the construction of a mound in the early 1700s, and historian Cadwallader Colden wrote in 1747 about a similar process involving a log structure burial inside an earth mound.[90] General George Rogers Clark, whose American colonial armies roamed the "western" territories, asserted that he had heard Natives' stories describing the mounds as the work of their forefathers. Thomas Jefferson carefully excavated a mound on his Monticello property and reported his findings in his 1787 *Notes on the State of Virginia*, in which he proclaimed that ancestors of the tribes with which he was familiar had built it:

> *The late discoveries of Captain Cook...have proved that if the two continents of Asia and America be separated at all, it is only by a narrow straight. So that from this side also, inhabitants may have passed into America: and the resemblance between the Indians of America and the Eastern inhabitants of Asia, would lead us to conjecture, that the former are descendants of the latter, or the latter of the former.*[91]

But other more fanciful theories, often based on common racism, conflicted with these prescient early observers. Edward Gibbon had published his *The Decline and Fall of the Roman Empire* in 1781, influencing thinkers of the time to focus on the classics as the basis of history. Author Jason Calavito notes that until the continents of the West had been encountered, the people of the Renaissance knew only Europe, Asia and Africa,[92] so all sorts of theories, often relying on biblical accounts, emerged to explain the people found on North and South America. Faith-based theorists posited that Native Americans must be descendants of Noah who discovered the New World in their wandering or that they were one of the "lost" tribes of Israel, scattered after the Babylonians destroyed Jerusalem. Spanish writers suggested the land itself had risen up from the sea as Atlantis, which had supported a supposed advanced civilization that fit nicely with the organized society required to construct complex earthworks. (This theory continues in modern literature.) As European explorers advanced farther into the North American continent, they reported that they encountered social groups made up of people with relatively light skin, light-colored hair and blue eyes. These, the scholars of the time explained, must have been leftovers from early Welsh colonists or Irish or English monks who crossed the Atlantic in search of souls and expanded their colonies to become great societies.

Writers at the junction of the eighteenth and nineteenth centuries began to expand the possibilities. Whereas Thomas Jefferson had offered plausible scholarly theory as to the continental origins of the mounds, French author Michel Guillaume Jean de Crevecoeur, King Louis XVI's consul to the United States and a friend of Jefferson's, took secondhand information to support his own thinking. He consulted with Benjamin Franklin about Jefferson's research after Franklin examined it himself, and then in his 1801 book *Voyage dans la Haute-Pensylvanie et dans l'état de New-York*, Crevecoeur freely and inaccurately copied from Franklin to corrupt Jefferson's ideas concerning the origin of North American earthworks. Crevecoeur corresponded with English botanist Benjamin Barton, who studied pottery from mounds and at first saw a connection with the Toltecs of Mexico and then changed his mind to support the Shawnee legend of the Moon-Eyed People, whom Barton described as nocturnal whites driven away in the distant past by the Shawnee. (In recent times, Mann said the Moon-Eyed People were simply mound builders who worshipped the moon and used it for timekeeping, hence a nocturnal lifestyle.)

In Ohio of the early 1800s, Caleb Atwater, legislator and postmaster of Circleville, surveyed a large, circular earthwork that had inspired the community's name. In "A Description of the Antiquities Discovered in the State of Ohio and Other Western States," delivered to the American Antiquarian Society, Atwater said such constructions were the work of "Hindoos," with pottery similar to that seen in India.[93] This theory informed the work of DeWitt Clinton, mayor of New York City and self-trained anthropologist, who had corresponded with Atwater in preparation of a report Clinton presented to the New York Historical Society in December

1811. In that speech, Clinton suggested a lost race constructed the mounds of New York, a theory he expanded in 1818, as governor of New York State, in a report to the Literary and Philosophical Society of New York.

The educated eastern establishment of the time was the first to hear these presentations by Atwater and Clinton, but wondrous accounts began to seep into the public consciousness with the invention of popular media in the years before the Civil War. One of the most widely read was *Traditions of De-coo-dah and Antiquarian Researches*,[94] published in 1858 by William Pidgeon, who claimed to have explored Serpent Mound in the 1830s and pried apart a stone altar there, prompting Squire and Davis a few years later to comment on an "ignorant visitor" who had despoiled the property. Pidgeon's fanciful recollections told the stories of De-coo-dah, an elderly Native American of the extinct Elk clan and a supposed wanderer among many Indigenous communities. De-coo-dah, according to Pidgeon, described the source of the mounds as ancient inhabitants of the continent who built mounds and earthworks to commemorate events. For example, the earthworks of Fort Ancient, a large hilltop enclosure in southwestern Ohio, were constructed to celebrate the moon, De-coo-dah said. Pidgeon concluded that the builders of all the monuments in the Mississippi and Ohio Valleys—the Elk Nation, according to De-coo-dah—could not have been the recognized Natives, whom he described as slow and lazy, but must have descended from Europeans in the North and Mexicans in the South.

Newspapers, magazines and publishers of the time eagerly sought such strange content. Unfortunately, imaginative writers described ancient civilizations' exotic leftovers, suggesting mounds filled with treasures. Farmers and landowners of early America had generally considered mounds and earthworks as merely obstacles to be plowed under or around, but when word began to spread about potential buried riches, common folk and pseudo-researchers took pick and shovel to the mounds. In one example, landowners battled over possession of property in Wisconsin near Milwaukee that included effigy works, until eventually townspeople invaded the earthworks, removed their contents and sold the plunder. A generation later, residents of Charleston, Missouri, made thousands of dollars selling artifacts from mounds.[95] Into this environment Squire and Davis, with their scientific exploration and first publication of the Smithsonian, preserved illustrations of the earthworks while agriculture and crude, undisciplined digging continued to destroy them.

However, even Squire and Davis in their carefully organized research concluded that the works had been built by some lost civilization. Having examined earthworks from Florida to Wisconsin, they suggested the construction required organized society, probably agricultural. While they avoided making a direct connection to a vanished culture, they wrote:

> *We may venture to suggest that the facts thus far collected point to a connection more or less intimate between the race of the mounds and the semi-civilized nations which formerly had their seats among the sierras of Mexico, upon the plains of Central America and Peru, and who erected the imposing structures...invest the central portions of the continent with an interest no less absorbing than that which attaches to the valley of the Nile.*[96]

Squire and Davis dug into numerous mounds to unearth artifacts and human remains that they catalogued, but it was left to Frederic Putnam to invent the science of archaeology at his examination of the Serpent Mound works. Putnam's crews carefully cut into the serpent and found the ancient builders' willful preparation of the land. In digging nearby, the would-be archaeologists unearthed numerous artifacts and human burials. Putnam surmised that some of the near-surface interments held the remains of more recent peoples, while deeper tombs showed more antiquity. Further digging in mounds at the site exposed several other graves, including the one covering two decapitated skeletons. "The largest number of objects I have ever seen in a single grave was found with those skeletons," Putnam wrote.[97]

In total, near the Serpent Mound, Putnam and his workers exposed almost two dozen graves and hundreds of artifacts. "The outlines of a picture have been traced out," Putnam said, adding that it would require further archaeological and geological work to fill in the texture of the cultures that had used the serpent site. For himself, Putnam suggested that the area around the serpent was a place of gathering for "ceremonies of great importance" but never a thriving community. Nor could he bring himself to make a connection with historical Indigenous cultures. In his opinion, people had come to the serpent for "special religious rites connected with the older faiths, which, so far as we know, had their greatest development in Asia, which is the land, more than any other, that we have reason to consider as the original home of...one of the early peoples of America."[98]

By the mid-twentieth century, however, other scholars began to believe that people known to the first white explorers considered the location a sacred shrine. However, eventually it became overgrown, its significance lost in memory. Recollection was left to Emerson F. Greenman, an archaeologist who in 1934 determined that Putnam's archaeology had exposed the work

Large mound south of the serpent effigy in Serpent Mound State Memorial. *Author photo.*

of the Adena people,[99] a culture defined by the writing of Ohio State Archaeological and Historical Society curator William C. Mills. In 1901, Mills had signed a contract to scientifically analyze the content of a well-known earthwork near Chillicothe, Ohio, where railroad construction threatened a twenty-four-foot-tall conical earthwork on the estate named "Adena" by Thomas Worthington, Ohio's first governor. When Mills's crews opened the mound, they found thirty-three individuals had been interred there with an assortment of artifacts that Mills thoroughly catalogued, including copper rings, beads, spear and arrow heads, a shell animal ornament and a magnificent clay pipe in the shape of a human.[100] A generation later, Greenman judged the artifacts similar to those found in the oblong mound a few yards south of the Great Serpent and called it "probable" that the culture that built the Adena mound in Chillicothe had also raised the burial mound near the serpent. In 1943, James B. Griffin of the University of Michigan dated the Serpent Mound–area artifacts to what he called an Adena culture.[101] Two years later, University of Kentucky anthropologists William S. Webb and Charles Snow, in their detailed two-volume study of the Adena people, carefully compared ceramics fragments and made the conclusion unambiguous: "The Great Serpent Mount [*sic*] of Ohio is now believed to be of Adena origin."[102]

The archaeologists who studied the earthworks at the Great Serpent Mound could describe burial patterns, artifacts and construction methods in great detail, but they could not scientifically link this knowledge to periods in western history. It remained for archaeologist William Romain to try. In the late 1970s, he associated known dates of total solar eclipses that crossed over the promontory area above Brush Creek to construction of the Great Serpent earthwork, which he took to be a fabulous snake in the act of swallowing the disk of the sun. He found three dates, ranging from about 800 BCE to AD 100, that matched his criteria, but various factors clouded the precision of the measurement.[103]

Across all archaeological research, more precise guesses as to the age of sites required the application of radiocarbon-14 dating, which measures the molecular deterioration of carbon in organic material. By the 1950s, radiocarbon measurement techniques allowed scientists to assign approximate dates to organic materials removed from diggings at earthworks, and in their 1957 second volume, authors Webb and Snow listed charcoal samples from various Adena works as dating to the period between roughly 1200 BC and AD 1500.

In 2011, renovation of a restroom building and installation of utilities at Serpent Mound Park gave the Ohio Historical Society an opportunity to again seriously study the grounds. The organization hired ASC Group, Inc., a cultural resource firm in Columbus, Ohio, which scoured the area south of the serpent effigy with archaeological digs under guidance of the National Historic Preservation Act of 1966. ASC found many artifacts, including stone tools and ceramic pieces, in the soil below the topsoil level that dated to the Adena culture, around 200 BC. "The Adena were living in this location and carrying out various domestic activities," wrote researcher Daniel Weintraub.[104] The study also determined that the ashy condition of the soil showed long-term use.

The ash in this ancient soil layer also yielded a piece of charcoal, which was submitted for carbon dating. This revealed that the artifact dated to the period between AD 1041 and 1211, a time of the Fort Ancient culture. The ASC group concluded that the dimensions and characteristics of the burned area showed likely long-term ritual activity. "This finding is quite significant," the ASC group wrote. "It indicates the continued use of the area surrounding the conical mound long after Adena occupation of the site."[105]

Subsequent researchers in recent times turned frequently to radiocarbon-14 techniques to determine more precisely when people gathered to build Serpent Mound. Those investigations, however, illustrated both the strengths and weaknesses of carbon-14 dating techniques: rather than giving a more defined range of years when Serpent Mound was raised, radiocarbon dating prompted disputes and controversy that continue to this day.

Chapter 8

WHAT SCIENCE SAYS TODAY

A critique of a Serpent Mound map led scientists to apply up-to-date analysis to its interior. Research by the Hardmans hinted that the undulations of the Great Serpent pointed to the summer and winter solstices,[106] but subsequent studies questioned the accuracy of those results. According to archaeologists Robert Fletcher and Terry Cameron, writing in 1986, restorations by Putnam and then the Depression-era CCC altered the shape of the earthwork so much that it was necessary to find the original foundation of the earthwork. Thus, Fletcher and Cameron initiated a study in 1991 during which teams of Wright State University students first used ground-penetrating radar to confirm the shape of the earthwork and then, during a project to remove steps over the mound installed by the CCC, the Ohio Historical Society's Bradley Lepper (who had been a member of the Fletcher and Cameron team) sifted through its dirt and drilled into the mound to examine soil samples. Radiocarbon dating of an oak charcoal piece he had drawn from deep within the mound, far below the more modern backfill, indicated the wood had been buried between AD 1000 and 1140.[107]

That finding ignited a storm of controversy. Calling Lepper's results surprising, in 2011 a team of eight geologists and archaeologists from Ohio, Indiana, Nebraska and West Virginia used a core drilling device about an inch thick to pierce the effigy eighteen times to a depth of about six feet. They found what they believed to be an abandoned effigy coil near the "head" of the serpent and dug a trench in it, ultimately concluding that "the mound could have been constructed any time after 300 B.C.," but they admitted that the previous work by Fletcher "is generally convincing." The 2011 group compromised:

> *We propose that Serpent Mound was constructed and then later modified during two distinct episodes: an Adena construction about 2,300 years ago during which the mound was first built, followed about 1,400 years later by an episode of...renovation or repair.... The reason for renovating Serpent Mound 900 years ago is unknown, but might relate to repairs necessary after parts of the mound were damaged as a result of erosion, sinkhole subsidence, or both.*[108]

Lepper, in a late 2017 report, questioned the methods of that research team. He said early guesses as to the age of the Great Serpent relied on its relationship to the nearby mounds, a problem because of the many cultural artifacts associated with them. The work by Herrmann, et al., yielded incorrect dates because the researchers didn't take the content of the soil beneath the effigy into account. Further, Lepper wrote, the assertion that the Adena built the snake effigy isn't accurate because the Adena had few references to serpents, whereas the later Mississippian cultures created many serpents in artworks, artifacts and earthworks. This iconography illustrated a relationship between the First Woman and the Great Serpent, Lepper said.

John R. Haskell, writing for the Indigenous Peoples Research Foundation in 2016, made further guesses as to the date for construction of Serpent Mound and the culture or cultures that raised and used the effigy. He suggested that the serpent motif actually represents a dragon symbol common in Far Eastern cultures. He supports this hypothesis by tracing faint marks that represent birds and faces, recognized in Far Eastern art, in the cliff adjacent to the Serpent Mound site and by pointing out a mound in southern Indiana that appears similar to the familiar "yin and yang" motif of eastern philosophy.[109]

In a 2018 report, Lepper continued to use both iconography and radiocarbon dating to explain his evidence of Serpent Mound's age. First, he said that the serpent motif is not common in Adana culture, but people about one thousand years later employed animal motifs such as the smaller and more obscure effigy Alligator Mound to represent the Underwater Panther commonly associated with the serpent. "I reaffirm Fletcher and colleague's original assessment that Serpent Mound was a Fort Ancient expression of this broader Mississippian trend [that is, related to the great Cahokia mound complex in what is now Illinois] and suggest that its builders, indeed, may have been influenced by the Effigy Mound culture," Lepper said.[110]

For his second point, Lepper emphasized that radiocarbon examination of the charred oak samples showed a date of around 1200 CE. Older bits found and dated by previous researchers may have come from the remains of much earlier campfires dug up when the serpent builders sought earth to build their effigy, he said.

Archaeologist William Romain reacted quickly. In a response published in the same issue of an archaeological journal, he decried Lepper's accusation that his earlier writing had been "aggressively hostile."[111] Romain then referred to Putnam at work in 1888 and wrote that Lepper's samples had come from earth heaped back onto the earthwork in Putnam's restoration or during the CCC work to build steps in the 1930s. He further refuted Lepper's observation that the Serpent Mound area had few drainage problems that would have washed out portions of the serpent and made work for Fort Ancient–age repair crews.

Romain then turned to Lepper's claim that icons of serpents rarely showed up in Adena artifacts but frequently in Fort Ancient works. "The serpent was likely important in the cosmology of Eastern Woodlands people going back thousands of years," Romain wrote, adding that a dispute involving counting serpents in archaeological digs "becomes silly."[112] Further, he said, applying modern beliefs to unearthed artifacts reminded him of pseudoscientific "ancient alien" theorists who claim that extraterrestrial beings "seeded" Earth's first cultures and then annihilated themselves in aerial warfare. In conclusion, Romain suggested Lepper had chronology backward: the Late Woodland peoples—the Fort Ancient culture—took their cues from the earlier Adena Serpent Mound.[113]

Geologist G. William Monaghan and geoarchaeologist Edward W. Herrmann again compromised, suggesting that Adena peoples initially built the serpent and after a period of several hundred years a Fort Ancient culture modified it. Monaghan and Herrmann had driven cores into the earthwork, compared the different layers of earth and discussed Putnam's 1880s assertion that the serpent's builders stripped the original soil before adding new dirt. Charcoal bits that remained after natural forest fires may have been reintroduced at that time, according to samples in the cores read by the researchers, but then there was a large gap in the cores before more charcoal bits appeared. "We can settle the chronology of Serpent Mound by revisiting it as a team (including Lepper); pushing new cores...and reopening several more of Putnam's trenches," Monaghan and Herrmann wrote.[114]

A year later, Lepper responded to the question of snakes. "In contrast to the abundance of serpent imagery in the Fort Ancient cultures, there is a nearly complete absence of serpent imagery in Adena iconography," he wrote.[115] Lepper and colleagues continued the study of iconography when they connected the Wisconsin area's widespread effigy mounds and rock art, which dated to around AD 1000, to the message of Serpent Mound and to Alligator Mound.[116] These mounds, they said, represented fertility symbols brought by people fleeing severe drought in the Mississippi area to verdant valleys in the East that had not experienced drought.[117] The migrants brought with them new artistic patterns and new concepts: stories of First Woman, the Great Serpent, the Underwater Panther and other creatures that resurrected humankind.

Lepper rejoined this debate with a discussion published in 2020 in which he noted Danish research that identified weaknesses in carbon-14 dating processes. Radiocarbon dates from soil in eighteen Danish mounds revealed unexpectedly old samples, so the Danish researchers "used the same procedures to obtain new dates for mounds that already had been dated by more reliable means."[118] Results showed that carbon dating added about seven hundred years to samples that already had been dated by dendrochronology, the well-accepted study of tree rings. Those European researchers suspected that supposedly old charcoal could survive unaffected in topsoil for thousands of years, so Lepper extended that to suggest topsoil might have been burned off by early Adena workers, as Putnam's excavations suggested, leaving burned substances that remained for years, well into the Fort Ancient habitation at the Serpent Mound area.

Lepper in 2022 proposed another link to the Late Woodland culture, and thus the later date for the effigy's construction, when he wrote, "The idea that Serpent Mound might incorporate multiple solar alignments in its design… provides additional support for a Fort Ancient culture affiliation for the Serpent."[119] He reiterated a connection to rock art and fertility symbolism that showed a "Path of Souls/Milky Way, along which the souls of the dead travel on their journey to the Realm of the Dead.…The belief that the Milky Way is the 'highway to heaven' is nearly universal among the Indigenous tribes of North America."[120] He concludes that the Great Serpent Mound, which he describes as "overwhelming as a landscape experience," combines Late Woodland and Mississippian cultures.[121]

In 2023, Sandra Garner, an anthropologist at Miami University of Ohio, wrote extensively about Serpent Mound and the monumental Newark Earthworks about fifty miles northeast in response to numerous and questionable popular television commentaries about the earthworks. Both sites had been nominated for the UNESCO World Heritage site status, and although the television shows and a documentary, *Lost Civilizations of North America*, brought throngs of visitors and attention to southern and central Ohio, the programs referenced all sorts of New Age, ancient alien and mystic theories not recognized by the scholarly community.

Garner says that in reality, the Indigenous population had been decimated first by tribal warfare, then disease brought to the New World by Europeans and finally by exile enforced by settlers. This atmosphere of elimination destroyed the memory of mythology and rituals of the cultures that produced both Serpent Mound and earthworks of the Ohio Valley. When Chief Glenna Wallace of the Eastern Shawnee Tribe of Oklahoma, one of the groups that claims the Ohio Country as homeland territory, was taken on a tour of the Newark Earthworks in 2007, she expressed surprise by their size and complexity; she had heard of Serpent Mound but not of the Newark Earthworks.[122] As Garner says, "It was likely that [Chief Wallace's] distant ancestors had built the mounds and she, a descendant, had not even known they existed."[123]

Garner recognizes that the Adena, the Hopewell and the Fort Ancient cultures inhabited the Ohio Valley and advanced through increasingly sophisticated lifestyles. Over time, these societies shifted from hunter-gatherer lifestyles and horticulture to organized agriculture, as shown by research that confirms difficult-to-grow food plants were imported by the Fort Ancient people into the Ohio Valley from western sources and cultivated,[124] while ceremonial earthworks became complex and monumental. In fact, researcher James R. Duncan says that by the Middle Woodland period (approximately 1000 BC to AD 1000), improved agriculture and exchange of seed stock and woman-oriented social activities "gives rise to the canonical depiction of many spirit beings" (that is, earthwork effigies), especially the First Woman and the Great Serpent. Duncan says he believes that by AD 600, "post–Middle Woodland societies continued to exchange seeds and gardening techniques with neighboring groups," but subsequent fast-growing populations "caused friction among groups as competition for territory increased…and, secondly, introduction of the bow and arrow added to cultural stress."[125]

Archaeologist and historian Peter Topping of the University of Newcastle in England adds another element to the social instability. He writes that mound construction would have required large numbers of people from disparate clans or communities, and organizing these groups would have required "potentially polarizing socio-economic systems" and ceremonial displays of wealth or power. "Such differences may have been used to define and maintain separate cultural identities," he says.[126] In other words, dividing society into leaders and followers, or upper and lower classes, would have been a further cultural stress that probably helped dissipate Native American culture.

Eventually, white settlers inhabited the Ohio Valley in their colonization, although "settler colonists could not mentally link these astounding achievements [of earthwork construction] to the local indigenous inhabitants."[127] The Shawnee, the Miami, the Delaware and other Native peoples, dispossessed of their homelands, had lost their cultural connection to the mythology that created the earthworks.

According to Garner, the settlers of the Ohio region recognized the architectural achievements of the earthworks but failed to understand the ceremonial significance of them. Because no one now speaks for the Native Americans who defined the sacred space at Serpent Mound, that puzzlement seems to continue to today. Various groups have stepped into the void in attempts to define the goals established by the UNESCO World Heritage designation that seeks to preserve world culture. In the case of the Serpent Mound application, its goals prioritize Native American representation, which prompts conflict with assorted groups such as the Friends of Serpent Mound, fundamentalist Christians and New Age believers who see the Serpent Mound site as a center of energy located on a "ley line," an esoteric belief in earth energies and for some a guide for alien spacecraft. Speaking for the Friends of Serpent Mound group (an organization originated with the Adams County tourism bureau and not officially affiliated with Serpent Mound State Memorial), executive director Delsey Wilson says she does not see how the controversies may be resolved.[128]

Chapter 9

VOICES FROM BEFORE HISTORY

About nine hundred years ago, people visited the Great Serpent regularly to peer into the night sky with great celebration. Modern observers generally agree that Indigenous people created Serpent Mound as a ceremonial site, but those who study the effigy debate continuously the purpose and age of the Great Serpent Mound. Archaeology writer Clifford Richey says it seems very likely that the Ohio Serpent Mound was a cosmological statement similar to the Mayan Glyphs of Central America and the Nazca compositions of Peru,[129] which, like Serpent Mound, can only be truly appreciated from the air. In Utah, petroglyph drawings show a serpent with mouth agape and curled tail, a conceptualization remarkably similar to Ohio's serpent. Widespread Indigenous cultures recognized a mythological serpent, illustrated by intact snake depictions in the Archaic-aged (1000 BCE) cliff dwellings of the Honanki Heritage Site of the Red Rock area near Sedona, Arizona.

But the rituals of Serpent Mound left no traces that can be sifted out by archaeology, and guesses as to the form of celebrations are made at peril. Ethnologist Mann warns, "Simply plopping mangled tradition into the discussion as generically 'Indian,' leaving it shorn of the associational matrix peculiar to its nation of origin, is disingenuous and not very helpful."[130] Because scholars acting outside of Indigenous cultures have colonial, imperial and racial biases, to really understand all the studies, modern observers must recognize "the disenfranchisement of indigenous peoples," mythology scholar Charlotte Moroz says.[131] Linguist Jay Miller

Above: Archaic-era small snake drawing on a rock wall near Sedona, Arizona. *Author photo.*

Opposite: Prehistoric large snake image on a rock wall near Sedona, Arizona. *Author photo.*

goes even further: "Outsiders, especially academics, lack any fuller sense of cultural context."[132]

Nevertheless, some westerners have made efforts to learn, and Indigenous writers have tried to explain, the mythology that incorporates the Great Serpent Mound. The first and most flamboyant of the white people to attempt to explain Serpent Mound may have been William Pidgeon, who before the American Civil War related at great length and with substantial fiction the pronouncements of the Sioux elder De-coo-dah. According to Pidgeon, De-coo-dah "stated that this union of symbols originated in the fact that both were inseparably associated as objects of worship…and that those earthen symbols were arranged in the relative position of those selected in the heavens."[133] De-coo-dah's interpretation illustrates how stories have been transmitted by the web of oral tradition, so mythologists, like linguists studying languages, can trace the fundamentals of stories passed along in spoken stories. Thus, according to the widespread oral heritage of Indigenous cultures, the world comprised three layers: the upper sky, which is the realm of birds, clouds and stars; the middle earth, home of humans and animals; and the lower layer, including the waters. The Cherokee, the Lenape and other cultures say the respected "Uktena," the Keen-eyed, the Great Horned Serpent, rules the dark underworld in Indigenous mythologies, opposing the "Above World" with thunder, lightning, eclipses, earthquakes and other earthly manifestations of instability.[134]

Perhaps these observations help explain the *why* behind the Serpent Mound's construction. In Indigenous traditions, the iconography and mythology of the serpent were well known as sources of hidden knowledge, and the creators of Serpent Mound, people who lived in close harmony with the natural world, must have recognized the power of their serpent effigy when they placed it in a celestial relationship between the sky above and the underworld below. "A monumental earthwork constructed in the shape of a serpent is not likely to have existed in a cultural vacuum," says Lepper.[135] English historian Topping suggests widely recognized cultural beliefs in the societies of the Indigenous peoples may explain why they put so much care, planning and hundreds of hours of effort into building an effigy that may have remained as a "vacant ceremonial center" between special events. "The role of such ceremonial centres [*sic*] must have been crucial in cementing alliances and maintaining group identity amongst what were otherwise small, dispersed communities," he writes.[136]

The impetus to raise earthworks, rather than burial mounds, may have come around AD 800, when Dhegihan Sioux language groups seem to have experienced a spiritual revival centered on belief in the First Woman and the First Man.[137] Alice Fletcher, the woman who collected money in Boston for Frederic Putnam, lived among Native Americans in the American Midwest and reported their beliefs. She said that according to tradition, the First Woman and First Man ancestral beings had absorbed the eternal spirit and shared their blessings through sacred bundles carried on each individual's person[138] or in shrines including mounds and effigies. When members of the people we call the Fort Ancient culture fled drought conditions in the West and migrated to the Ohio Valley's verdant forests, they brought with them respect for one of the most recognized icons, the Great Serpent.

Mythology scholar Moroz offers her own guess as to the purpose embedded in Serpent Mound: "It seems clear to me that the mythologies of the Serpent Mound are linked to the human being in-tune with celestial timing."[139] Indigenous author and ethnologist Mann, citing the work of the Clark and Marjorie Hardman research team, recognizes the snake effigy as an observatory, with the head of the snake pointing to summer solstice sunset and undulations of the snake effigy pointing to the spring and fall solstices. The archaeology team of Hardman and Hardman, in their efforts to more accurately map Serpent Mound, determined the purposeful direction of the curves, while the altar in the center of the oval took an important function. "Our [own] culture places importance on an altar," they said. "...The altar or the vicinity of the altar would mark an observation point for sunset summer solstice."[140] Romain adds that the end of the curled tail, when aligned with the nose of the serpent, forms a direct line to true north.

These guesses suggest yearly ceremonies in tune with celestial alignments. Moroz adds detail:

> *It seems clear that the builders of Serpent Mound held wide visions of the cosmos and their place within it, performing rituals of music and dance, practices based upon the premise of harmony, all with the objective to honor the immense forces which gift us the dance of life and death, the dance between seasons, between night and day, offering a space for integration and union. Perhaps the serpent is eating the egg at its jaws, perhaps Scorpius is ingesting the sun, but is this not an image of union and blending, becoming the other or opposite? What better metaphoric companion to the mound practices than music, which models celestial timing, rhythm and harmony, all speaking not to the helplessness but to the vital role humanity plays in tuning to and tuning the world above and below.*[141]

Interesting recent studies have added to the *how* of Serpent Mound. Ohio archaeologists Jamie L. Davis and Jarrod Burks and anthropologist Elliott Abrams applied a method called architectural energetic analysis to the construction of Serpent Mound when they compared photographs shot by Putnam at his discovery of the effigy to images shot after his "restoration" of the effigy. They determined that Putnam and his crews, in their effort to restore the earthwork to its "original" size, had increased its height but not its width. The many studies that have dug into the serpent all showed it was raised using the same yellowish-brown clay and soil on which it sat, indicating the material was not imported from elsewhere, although its original height could only be surmised.

To study the amount of work that went into it, Davis, an unmanned remote aerial system (drone) expert, carefully surveyed the effigy from about sixty yards in the air using photogrammetry software that created a digital surface model of Serpent Mound. That image allowed the viewers to study a simulation of a three-dimensional view of the effigy without grass or other obstructions and make measurements showing a cross-section of the mound as a semicircular shape and roughly 20 feet wide at its base and 3 feet tall, on average. That information multiplied by the 852-foot length of the serpent's body, minus the "egg" and "jaws" of the creature, came to a total volume of about 1,202 cubic meters, or 1,572 cubic yards, of earth, the equivalent of about five full medium-sized dump trucks.

For the next step, the trio of archaeologists turned to research on energetics (that is, the amount of human work required to build a structure). Because

Serpent Mound illustration. *From* The Serpent Mound, Adams County, Ohio: Mystery of the Mound and History of the Serpent, *2nd ed., 1907.*

of the studies that have shown the entire effigy is composed of generally one type of soil, the researchers assumed that all of it had been scraped up from the area adjacent to the existing mound, an average distance of about a football field from the effigy site to places where the builders would have encountered different soil types. They noted that the ancient planner or planners had removed topsoil to expose the shape of the effigy, after which over some brief period workers piled earth on the site. "It is possible that the entire Serpent Mound was constructed in one episode," the researchers write, with the explanation that distinctions in layers within the mound probably come from different loads rather than from different times, because evidence shows no topsoil from vegetation growth and decomposition had developed between layers.[142]

The researchers guessed that "building activities only involved quarrying the soil, then transporting and depositing that soil at the site of construction." They called this work "significant," however, because energetics studies that attempted to closely replicate tools and soil types typical of those at Serpent Mound have suggested a single worker could move a little more than about two cubic yards of soil per day, the equivalent of two full standard bathtubs. The researchers further calculated that if they were toting the soil an average distance of about three hundred feet from borrow pits to the mound dump site, it would take about 1,300 person-days to fill the volume of Serpent Mound.

The authors turned to studies showing that societies of the time when Serpent Mound was constructed lived in small communities of about 12 persons scattered across the countryside. Because their research suggests people constructed the effigy rather quickly, the researchers guess that several communities banded together for the Serpent Mound project, perhaps in a ceremonial celebration. Simple calculations show that if sixty-five small hamlets provided a few people each so that there were 259 workers, they could raise the effigy in a mere five days. Conversely, "In the longest construction scenario, the construction of Serpent Mound occurred in a five-day construction period annually for five consecutive years, involving some 52 people from 13 hamlets," the researchers wrote.[143]

Comparison with other earthworks in the Ohio Valley suggests the Serpent Mound project was a much larger task than usual. "From the architectural energetics perspective of Serpent Mound...we infer that far more participants from a broader region constructed Serpent Mound." The trio of scientists warn, however, that some Hopewell-era earthworks of the area dwarf the serpent. For example, the Octagon and Observatory Circle earthworks of Newark, Ohio, about fifty miles northeast of Serpent Mound State Memorial and among the largest wall enclosures in the world, "have a volume roughly 20 times larger than Serpent Mound."[144] The researchers cite some scholars who say such large projects may have involved great numbers of people, perhaps pilgrims, meeting to work for several days annually. Ultimately, such work

> *reflects the ability for dozens of small hunter-gatherer/horticultural communities to aggregate and work together on a collective project with a singular unifying purpose. Further, this analysis indicates that small communities of dispersed hamlets were capable of organizing for the purpose of building a communal structure, drawing participants from a distance to do so. The implication is that dispersed communities need to create and maintain bonds that unify, bonds that remind people of their shared history in times of plenty as well as times of scarcity.*[145]

Chapter 10

VOICES IN THE PRESENT AND THE FUTURE

Today, Native Americans, having been ripped from their ancestry, complain that their lack of presence in modern society keeps them from having a definitive voice in interpretation of effigies and earthworks, including Serpent Mound. They note that modern scientific conclusions about the people who raised the mounds are based on the work of early curiosity seekers and later archaeologists whose chief methods often relied on excavations, which are in fact grave robbing. While the artifacts from the digs have provided valuable clues regarding the earliest cultures of North America, the remains of ancestors of Indigenous people often rest in museums today.

Misunderstanding between the scientific community and Indigenous people has a long history. Native American scholar and writer Vine Deloria Jr. said the misunderstanding centers in three areas: "While it may appear that Indians are adopting the values and practices of American culture, in science, in religion, and in forms of social interaction—most prominently government—there is still a tremendous gap between the beliefs and the practices of both whites and Indians."[146]

In fact, the lack of coordination extends to even the most basic of elements, that of defining just who is a Native American. The Indian Reorganization Act of 1934 recognized three classes of person as "Indian": 1) Members of any recognized Indian tribe now under federal jurisdiction. As of the year 2000, this included 570 such groups, according to Deloria; 2) All persons who are members of such groups living within the boundaries of a reservation; 3) All other persons one-half or more of Indian blood (regardless of tribal regulations).[147]

Cultural and religious misunderstandings have been at the heart of social and scientific conflicts. The earliest researchers, curiosity seekers and pseudoscientists viewed items dug out from burial mounds and graves as items of interest; Native Americans were aghast at the practice, regardless of who did the digging. The U.S. Congress acted to pass the Antiquities Act of 1906 to protect archaeological sites and said that artifacts declared "archaeological resources" could be excavated and sent to museums. Author Kathleen Fine-Dare says, "According to one estimate, by 1990 at least 14,500 Native American bodies were in the hands of federal agencies."[148] In response to this wholesale removal of Indigenous culture, the Historic Sites Act of 1935 created a national board that advised the federal government regarding historic sites, buildings and monuments, and under its authority, the first repatriation of Native American artifacts took place in 1938.[149]

In response to grievances stirred by cultural and social disputes, in the 1920s, Native Americans founded several organizations to encourage political activism and represent the interests of Native Americans battling narrow-minded legislation in Congress. After World War II, returning Native American veterans came home with a greater sense of Native American commonwealth, and many became active in the National Congress of American Indians (NCAI). Founded in 1944, the NCAI "continues to be one of the most influential Indian rights organizations in the United State and has contributed a great deal to discussions regarding repatriation matters."[150]

The end of World War II also brought capital revitalization efforts such as urban renewal and the interstate highway system that threatened many historic places. In an effort to preserve the country's historic heritage, Congress passed the 1966 National Historic Preservation Act, which defined "historic sites," strengthened the National Register of Historic Places, established state historic preservation offices and gave the secretary of the interior power to pursue World Heritage status for some historic places. Native American tribes and leaders were added to the list of consultants in 1986, a double-edged sword because while it included representation, it placed the burden of proof for cultural or sacred authenticity on the tribes.

By the mid-1960s, the American Indian Movement (AIM) was using modern news media manipulation and social activism to bring Native American issues to public consciousness, and in 1971, the Second Convention of Indian Scholars aired issues of questionable museum practices relative to artifacts and human remains. This initiated the thinking that ultimately led to Public Law 101-601, the Native American Graves Protection and Repatriation Act of 1991 (NAGPRA).

The 101st Congress of the United States formulated NAGPRA following long-term lobbying by the National Congress of American Indians and other Native American groups and passed it into law, signed by President George Bush, on November 16, 1990. Indigenous groups not only lauded the new law but also recognized its weaknesses. NAGPRA fortifies prohibitions against the sale, purchase and transport of human remains and religious artifacts and establishes procedures for appropriate consultation and practices in archaeological work that involves Native American cultural artifacts. It calls for inventory of cultural materials and human remains in museums and research collections in preparation for repatriation of them to appropriate Native American groups. "Inadvertent discovery" of cultural artifacts or remains must be addressed with appropriate procedures, and civil penalties, in dollar amounts, were published.

On the other hand, Native Americans recognize that the law applies only to agencies and institutions that have federal connections or are on federal land. NAGPRA, as well as federal and state laws, prohibits sale or purchase of any human remains, but should a culturally important artifact such as a "medicine bundle" be traded on private land—for example, in Adams County outside the grounds of Serpent Mound State Memorial during summer solstice festivals—no laws are being broken. In addition, NAGPRA calls for repatriation of items, but its regulations as to who gets them are nebulous: the question of "standing" vexes the courts when decisions must be made regarding repatriation[151] because in eighteen eastern states, for example, the federal government does not recognize any Native American tribes. Lacking substantial evidence, the question of lineal descendants or written records, necessary for repatriation under NAGPRA, becomes extremely difficult to answer.

Some archaeologists gnashed their teeth at the passage of NAGPRA. "The brutal truth is that the Society of American Archaeology roadblocked repatriation and reburial at every step," writes ethnologist Mann.[152] Gradually, however, scientists have adapted to the law's requirements. "NAGPRA has fundamentally changed the way American archaeology is practiced in the United States," writes University of Arizona anthropologist T.J. Ferguson.[153] And NAGPRA has forced both archaeologists and Native Americans to reconcile their differences in interpretation. Most archaeologists, who in the past looked beyond mythology and culture, now see the cultural connection to their research. As author Fine-Dare says,

"'Being Indian' can carry…a religious connotation, one that is crucial in understanding the importance of the repatriation movement and the difficulties many tribes are having with NAGPRA."[154]

Questions continue regarding the collections in a variety of realms because of the volume of collections. For example, while working at the Serpent Mound State Memorial grounds, Putnam and other subsequent researchers unearthed thousands of items that the scientists shipped back to sponsoring institutions, where they were measured, weighed, photographed and either stored or put on display. That was mostly in the days of the "invisible Indian," but with the emergence of Native American consciousness, activists continue to express horror at the dissoluteness of their ancestors' remains and treasured cultural artifacts; NAGPRA gives substantial legal foundation for the complaints.

The Peabody Museum, which received Putnam's findings from Serpent Mound State Memorial, has wrestled with the consequences of its collections. In a 2023 article in *The Harvard Gazette*, the official news outlet for Harvard University, Kelli Mosteller, executive director of the Harvard Native American Program, said, "It's important to understand that the scale of Harvard's involvement is different than many other institutions. There are thousands of ancestors in the collections, and they came to be there as a result of practices that were deeply disrespectful and damaging to Native communities." Jane Pickering, the director of the Peabody Museum, also said the museum recognizes that the scope of NAGPRA calls for "fundamental change to the structure, practices and values of the museum," to which Mosteller added that in consultation with the tribes, the Peabody has learned the limits of tribes' ability to physically take possession because of staffing issues or lack of physical land for reburial.[155]

The Ohio History Connection, which oversees management of all the earthworks and grounds at Serpent Mound State Memorial, has confronted a number of issues related to its own collections. After NAGPRA was put into effect in 1991, Native Americans criticized the organization for a ham-handed approach to dealing with modern Native Americans and repatriation and for defining most of its holdings as "culturally unidentifiable." The U.S. Senate's Committee on Indian Affairs cited OHC as a major offender, but in a communication with Senator Brian Schwartz, chairman of the committee, dated June 16, 2023, Megan Wood, the OHC's executive director and CEO, said, "For the past 10 to 15 years, we have shifted to conducting active consultations in order to culturally affiliate Ancestors and collections and be proactive in assisting Tribes to be able to make claims and rebury their

Ancestors." According to the letter, OHC had included a representative from a federally recognized tribe on its board of trustees, which established an American Indian Relations Policy, and staffed an office to oversee compliance with that policy.[156] That document explained the history of the Ohio Historical Society/Ohio History Connection relationship with Ohio Native Americans, observing that all tribes had been removed from the state by the 1840s and none exist in the state today. "One of the chief consequences of the Jacksonian Removal Era is the absence of Tribal Nations and Indigenous cultural practices on the landscape of Ohio," the policy states.[157] It describes best practices for consultation with Native American representatives; recognition of sites important to Indigenous populations; and repatriation of ancestral remains, funerary objects and cultural objects.

Despite these published efforts, ProPublica, an online investigative journalism site, cited the Ohio History Connection in 2023 for the size of its collection of unrepatriated Native American remains. In "The Repatriation Database," the news organization published a chart indicating "at least 7,167 remains not made available for return" and only "0.1 percent of more than 110,300 associated funerary objects available for return to tribes." The Ohio History Connection responded by admitting that the designation of "culturally unidentifiable" may have been used in the past to retain its collections, but "our institution just doesn't allow [that] any more." The organization, the response says, recognizes the connection of its archaeological collections to Indigenous American cultures and accepts its responsibility to consult with federally recognized Indian tribes "and listen as Tribes inform us about histories, homelands and items in the collections."[158]

Brad Lepper, the Ohio History Connection's chief archaeologist, insists that the modern representatives of Native American tribes seem satisfied with the efforts of the Ohio History Connection. "All the tribes we are working with are happy with us," he said. "We're not doing it as fast as the national NAGPRA wants us to. Many of these [questions] are complicated issues." Lepper explained that because there are no resident tribes in Ohio, repatriation is difficult. "For a long time NAGPRA limited repatriation only to the tribe with a direct relationship to the remains. With anything older than a thousand years it's very hard to know which tribe. It could have been many tribes." In Ohio, he explained, the answer may be to repatriate to a coalition of tribes to avoid the problem of deciding whether, for example, remains should go to the Shawnee or the Miami.

Lepper admits OHC has more than seven thousand human remains, but some collections are as small as a single tooth; few are complete skeletons.

("We have none of the human remains from Serpent Mound," he noted.) The challenge is to sort out ownership. "All the tribal members I work with want this to be a careful, deliberative process, not a rushed process," Lepper said. "They want to be sure they're burying their ancestors, not someone else's ancestors. They appreciate the careful work we're doing to make sure that's what happens."[159]

Chapter 11

UNSOLVABLE MYSTERIES

The mysterious nature of Serpent Mound inevitably invites all manner of speculation about its purpose. Explorers, settlers and scholars from the time they first encountered the effigy have offered theories from the prosaic to the bizarre, ranging from its use as a calendar to suggestions that humans lost their lives there in sacrificial events or for ceremonies by paranormal shamans.

Intellectual probes include those by Frederic Putnam, Serpent Mound's original scholar and the man whose work preserved the site. Upon unearthing in 1888 two headless human burials and evidence of cremation in mounds several hundred feet south of the snake effigy, Putnam guessed human sacrifice.[160] Researcher Romain lists many writers who suggest blood rituals at Serpent Mound, and some assumed the mass of boulders in the center of the "egg" had been an altar for ceremonial human sacrifice, with "victims tossed over the cliff to the creek below"; others mistakenly cited burials inside the effigy.[161] Modern researchers who suggest that outliers of the Mississippian culture constructed the effigy would therefore link it to the huge earthworks complex of Cahokia in modern-day Illinois, where human sacrifices have been uncovered and cultural artifacts depict severed heads, headless bodies and warfare.[162]

The geology of the Serpent Mound site adds to the mystique. In the nineteenth century, General James G.R. Forlong, a British civil engineer and comparative religions scholar, wrote:

> *Is there not something more than mere coincidence in the resemblance between the Loch Nell and the Ohio serpent, to say nothing of the topography of their respective situations? Each has the head pointing west, and each terminates with a circular enclosure, containing an altar, from which looking along the most prominent portion of the serpent, the rising sun may be seen. If the serpent of Scotland is the symbol of an ancient faith, surely that of Ohio is the same.*[163]

A few other earthworks exhibit similar traits. Community researchers in Boyd County, Kentucky, identified a 627-foot-long serpent constructed of mostly portable-sized sandstone rocks positioned on a point overlooking the Big Sandy River; recent investigations have revealed a serpent, dubbed the Kern Effigy, crudely built of stone about fifty miles west of Serpent Mound in what is now Warren County, Ohio, in the floodplain of the Little Miami River;[164] in Ontario, Canada, near Peterboro, researchers identified a small uncoiled snake mound; and in Wisconsin, serpents are depicted among numerous effigy mounds. The locations of these mounds lead observers to suspect all of them have cosmological significance, as some of them appear to have been built around the time of the arrival of Halley's Comet in 1066, an event celebrated in European tapestries. Experts who study the massive Cahokia center note that construction of Cahokia began abruptly in the AD 1050s, near the time of a 1054 supernova that could be seen for twenty-three days in daylight near the crescent moon, a celestial event recorded by Chinese astrologers.[165]

One cultural expert muses that a casual examination of the Milky Way star cluster suggests a widespread Native American connection with the sinewy shape of serpents in general. Herman Bender, a geologist and cultural landscape specialist, says effigy structures throughout the present-day United States convey over hundreds of generations the Algonquin-language traditions of the Great Serpent as a creature of the underworld, a pattern that he sees even as far away as Norse legends. Although he links most motifs to east–west celestial arrangements, whereas the Great Serpent Mound points to the northwest summer solstice, all of the effigies seem to share a common time frame and tradition. "Although [Serpent Mound] is not known to be or have meant to have been related to the Milky Way when constructed, its astronomical properties bear mentioning because they exhibit the astronomical knowledge and construction skills of its builders in their ability to design, build and align parts of the serpent to key events in the sky, a testament to their observational abilities," Bender says.[166]

Other thinkers have more philosophical ideas. Michel-Gerald Boutet, a Quebec, Canada, independent researcher in mythology, folklore and Native American studies, posits that Serpent Mound is bound up in understanding of the cosmos and myths of the Serpent, called *Msi-kinepikwa* in Shawnee, that can only be truly understood "in the context of native Amerindian cultural world view and mind set."[167] Indigenous cultures all knew flood myths, Boutet says, and they symbolically linked them to the Great Serpent, a creature of the water. In addition, they linked the snake to the cosmos in ways not understood by non-Indigenous cultures. This made the effigies such as Serpent Mound sacred, hallowed places that "can mirror the night skies and star patterns thus giving telltale information on the Amerindian traditional perception of constellations."

Whereas Boutet says modern viewers can interpret Serpent Mound if they see it through the eyes of Indigenous peoples, author William John Meegan argues that only special knowledge "beyond the jaundice[d] eye of the mundane" allows true understanding of the effigy.[168] Meegan, a religion and mythology specialist, says that Esotericism—Western Mystery Tradition—is the key to understanding Serpent Mound. This belief, Meegan writes, is universal: "The Esoteric Science is not indigenous to any one culture on the face of the earth,"[169] and the spiritual-minded who are willing to spend a lifetime of contemplation and meditation can truly understand transcendental concepts that explain Serpent Mound. Meegan says the cultures of the Indigenous peoples "in constructing Serpent Mound and the surrounding astrological sites [believed] in the embrace of the Great Spirit exactly as the Christians did on an esoteric level."[170] (Modern theologians and historians of early Christianity will recognize Meegan's Esotericism as essentially Gnosticism, the notion that salvation can be achieved only through special wisdom.) For Meegan, beliefs linked to the mystery of the Great Serpent Mound include mystical traditions of astronomy and the cosmos, numerology and astrology. From astronomy, Meegan sees a link in the Great Serpent Mound's topography with constellations such as the Great Bear; from numerology, he sees the effigy as patterned after a Universal Mathematical Matrix, which relates the seven swirls in the Great Serpent's tail to the Seven Light Chakras of the body in Hindu tradition; and from astrology, Meegan links the constellations Draco (the dragon), Ursa Major (the Great Bear) and Ursa Minor (the Little Bear) to the solstice and equinox alignments of the Serpent's undulations that were identified by Romain and others.

Serpent Mound's location fascinates Meegan. Romain's use of LIDAR exposed the geology of the Serpent Mound area on the edge of the meteor creator, and Meegan comments, "Created from out of the universe of stars and its stellar debris and right on the periphery inside the crater is SERPENT MOUND: incredible!"[171] The resulting topography places Serpent Mound on a peninsula between Brush Creek and East Creek, which Meegan sees as artificial, creating a landscape similar to the Sinai Peninsula of the Near East and reminiscent of the Great Sleeping Bear. This location he calls the Axis Mundi—the center of the world—of the mound builder culture, a "highly sophisticated civilization" that utilized an 18.6-year lunar calendar related to religious events in Native American cultures as well as Judaism, Christianity and Islam. Understanding that relationship is left to the student who seeks "the deeper esoteric mysteries of the Great Bear's mythological teachings, although that student would first have to prove his or her worthiness to obtain that knowledge."[172]

Philosopher and researcher Ross Hamilton, who lives in southwestern Ohio, holds similar views. For Hamilton, the Great Serpent Mound serves as a Rosetta Stone, a "repository of the ancient wisdom, the retrieval of which requires less of the objective reasoning and more the subjective."[173] In his book *The Mystery of the Serpent Mound,* Hamilton writes that his purpose is to demonstrate that the Serpent serves as a messenger of the ancient Mystery Tradition. Introduced to the serpent earthwork by the Great Serpent Mound chapter of the American Society of Dowsers, Hamilton determined to answer the questions of who designed it, who built it and why. "The Serpent may have been a central figure in a broader picture," he suggests.[174]

Like Charlotte Moroz and William Meegan, Hamilton warns that new ways of thinking, suggested to be necessary to truly understand Serpent Mound, almost certainly guarantee dismissal from accepted archaeological circles. Standard methods such as digging and carbon dating, Hamilton writes, "reflect the materialistic bias of the conservative branch of the archaeological community."[175] He says that archaeologists have declined to link Esoteric philosophic study even to Native American history.

For Hamilton, the Mystery Tradition arose about five thousand years ago, perhaps before the pyramids of Egypt. He suggests Pythagoras, the Greek proto-philosopher, and his followers applied mathematical and geometrical theory such as the golden section or golden mean and other ratio measures to the letters of the Greek alphabet, which Hamilton relates to the shape of the Great Serpent. These universal ratios and patterns guided construction of the Great Serpent Mound, Hamilton writes.

Hamilton suggests the builders of Serpent Mound viewed the constellation of Draco the dragon in the stars and transferred that pattern to some medium in order to copy it in grand scale. "Such a skill is a known trait among great artists, and this would place the design of the Great Serpent into the realm of high art," he writes, adding that the terrace on which the serpent was constructed "appears to have been custom-made for the earthwork."[176] His speculation continues into pre–Civil War theories and echoes the work of researchers Jason Jarrell and Sarah Farmer, whose book *Ages of the Giants* examines historical accounts of unearthing the remains of giants in midwestern mounds. Hamilton asks:

> *Was the great Serpent Mound created by a mysterious race, the end of whose lineage was the beginning of the Adena people? It is a little-known fact, and one rarely pursued by archaeologists, that the very early pre-Adena folk had members of very tall stature...capable of great exertions and doing wonders. Could such an ancient race have been instrumental in creating the Great Serpent Mound?*[177]

But Hamilton continues further into pre-history. He asks if the Adena-Hopewell people arose out of archaic times and, like the ancient Egyptians, exhibited exceptional technological, artistic and organizational skills before their culture evaporated. Or, he asks, "was there a far earlier historic period or otherworldly source that communicated this knowledge through symbols that arrived in both ancient America and in the ancient Near East?"[178] There are, he says, "unmistakable signs that either a real genius was effectively nurtured in Ohio's prehistory, or the people here were privy to a tradition of what could only be interpreted as truly insightful and of superior intellect."[179]

Hamilton says he received a vision that revealed an almost universal Native American belief in the Great Spirit, and many sites—most lost—featured natural beauty spots often coupled with energetic and spiritual forces. "I strongly feel that the Serpent Mound is among the most important of sacred sites," he writes, and "our Serpent Mound is the remnant of an ancient philosophic transmission."[180]

Chapter 12

CONCLUSIONS

Writer John Meegan flips ethnologist Barbara Mann's "savagist theory," which holds that Europeans have always believed Native Americans are "savages." Meegan, on the other hand, says, "The White Man was a savage in the American Indian mindset because he raped Mother Nature and chased them from their ancestral lands."[181] Indigenous people tried to educate the ignorant white savages with mythology, Meegan writes, but over time and turmoil, Native American shamans lost the true knowledge. Among that vanished intelligence are the secrets of the Great Serpent Mound.

Modern work is revealing those riddles, despite the belief held by Meegan, Charlotte Moroz and Ross Hamilton that only special belief and exceptional knowledge can expose them. Explorers as early as Squire and Davis in 1848 carefully documented the Great Serpent Mound and other earthworks, and fifty years later, Putnam meticulously catalogued the site. Science unknown to those earlier theorists has now proposed a timeline for the effigy but at the same time opened up new controversies. Archaeology has dismissed racist theories of wandering "lost" white civilizations while revealing that many Native American cultures raised mounds and earthworks over hundreds of generations, and now science has virtually reconstructed the Native American cultures that designed and constructed the elaborate earthworks. Artfully fashioned tools, points, pipes and ornaments, as well as ritual burials shamelessly robbed, testify to thoughtful lifestyles of people who lived within nature long before written history. The Native American Graves Protection and Repatriation Act of 1991 now requires federally funded agencies and museums to cooperate with Native American groups to protect such items and ultimately return them to their rightful descendants.

Putnam, in his seminal work on conical mounds a few hundred feet from Serpent Mound, unearthed tools, ornaments and artifacts from the cultures now known as the Adena and the Hopewell. According to subsequent researchers, a different society built nearby Serpent Mound and did not include in it any material goods, although its carefully laid foundation and layers show a great deal of planning and thought went into its construction. Its value, we now know, lies in cultural and mythological energy. As many modern analysts conclude, the serpent's form clearly and dramatically indicates important dates on the yearly calendar. The giant reptile is, as Mann says, an observatory.

As with most other earthworks in the Ohio Valley, the builders did not live in a village near the effigy or nearby mounds while they worked there, but there is evidence of a small Indigenous community near the Great Serpent. Likely the earliest people to wander into the area discovered the beautiful setting above the creek, with its view of the valley stretching far into the distance over what they couldn't have known was a meteor crater. "The unusual geomorphology of this area was obviously an attraction to local communities, which is demonstrated by the presence of two adjacent mounds attributed to the Adena, thus potentially pre-dating the serpent mound by many centuries," writes Topping, who adds, "clearly this location held a deep cultural resonance where spiritual matters and the construction of monuments to the dead coalesced."[182] Later groups, perhaps pilgrims driven by drought from the Cahokia community far to the west,[183] established small villages nearby and expanded the hallowed grounds to include a celestial observatory, because as farmers they needed a reliable calendar. The honored Uktena, the Keen-eyed, the Great Horned Serpent, served that purpose, and modern studies in architectural energetic analysis show that the work of building their effigy had to involve a number of households, clans or communities, perhaps in annual celebrations and certainly under some kind of organized social or class structure. To guess that any other ancient culture or machinery was necessary to construct the effigy is pure unfounded conjecture.

We now recognize that Native American cultures evolved over centuries from hunter-gatherers to sedentary farmers who grew an assortment of vegetables such as maize, beans and squash and traded in seeds for those crops. In fact, the selective, grain-oriented diet may have over time worked against the good health of the people who built the mounds and hastened their demise. Because Indigenous peoples as early as the Adena cultivated crops,[184] it makes sense that these farmers would create and utilize the Serpent calendar to indicate, probably with great holidays including ceremony, dance and singing, the time of year to plant their crops and then later to begin the harvest.

Before disease, warfare and Europeans dissipated their societies, the Lenape, Cherokee, Shawnee and Iroquois cultures that inherited the mounds celebrated the sun, moon and stars (sky medicine) and agriculture (earth medicine). Topping says the rituals incorporated origin myths that "created the links between the dead, their surviving relations and the spirit world, and would have created the legitimation to underpin kinship and clan-based networks."[185] According to Jay Miller, a researcher who studies Native American cultures, the carefully constructed mounds and earthworks show "community vitality" that created, and continues to create, sacred and peaceful spaces. In a welcoming plaque situated on the Serpent Mound site, Shawnee Chief Ben Barnes says, "Serpent Mound was purposefully built for a special, sacred purpose. I should think that anyone who views the Serpent will realize its sacredness and treat this place as they would a cathedral, synagogue or mosque. When we see this place, this is our holy ground."[186]

This belief system of the builders, their ancestors and their descendants imbues Serpent Mound and its accompanying earthworks with many layers of secrets about their origins, lifestyles and stories. To know more of these will require new methods beyond static research. Explains mythology scholar Moroz, "The mythologies of this site are multidimensional and require multidimensional study, so as to hold space for the sophisticated astronomical and cosmological wisdom contained in this and other indigenous earth works."[187]

The mounds, Jay Miller says, are activated and active as well: Indigenous informants teach that "mounds are believed to be resilient, holding reserves of power much like a charged battery releasing vitalities over eons."[188] It remains for modern visitors to detect and absorb that energy.

Afterword

VISIT SERPENT MOUND

From the time he first viewed Serpent Mound, archaeologist Frederic Putnam envisioned a restoration that would encourage relaxation and quiet contemplation. In nearly a century and a half since then, caretakers have in varying forms honored that vision, and today, visitors will find a remarkable, exotic landscape that can be both awe-inspiring and tranquil at the same time.

Just as Native Americans discovered thousands of years ago, modern travelers will find Serpent Mound State Memorial amid the wooded, rolling hills of Adams County in southern Ohio. Despite its isolation, the site can be found easily after a pleasant drive on good roads about seventy miles east of Cincinnati, Ohio, or one hundred miles south of Columbus. Its entrance appears rather abruptly on State Route 73, a two-lane road that traverses the northwest–southeast trail from Hillsboro to Portsmouth, Ohio, although the closest villages, both on Ohio Route 41, are Peebles to the south or Sinking Spring to the north. (The larger of these is Peebles, which features a couple motels and dining areas.)

Once on Route 73, watch for the park entrance, which exits north from the road about a football-field's distance after it spans a small bridge over Ohio Brush Creek, a popular canoeing stream. Access to the park follows a curving lane uphill about a quarter mile to the spacious parking area, from which you can see the largest conical mound on the grounds, CCC-era stone restroom buildings and the site headquarters and museum building. A walking tour of Serpent Mound State Memorial should begin at the

Closed historic observation tower in 2024. *Author photo.*

museum for literature and a map that will guide you past informative panels along a paved trail to the effigy earthworks.

Until it was closed for renovation in 2025, the steel Serpent Mound Observation Tower, built in 1908, gave observers an excellent view of the earthwork. It will be restored because it's considered a cultural icon, but until it's reopened, visitors will have to view the scene from below it, an elevated location that nevertheless gives a nice vision of the serpent's scale. A

View of Serpent Mound coils from mid-effigy looking toward the tail. The closed tower is to the left, and the stone dedication tablet is in the center of the photo. *Author photo.*

short walk to the left takes you to the serpent's coiled tail and a notch in the treescape that reveals a scene of the valley below. Visitors may wish to rest a moment to contemplate and gather energy, because the paved walkway continues on an undulating tour completely around the effigy for a half mile. You will see that the serpent uncoils not on a flat plain but on a rolling terrain from the coiled tail at the top to the gaping "mouth" and "egg" at the lower end, an elevation change of perhaps 40 feet over the 1,300-foot length of the serpent. An observation point near the head of the serpent gives another view of the valley below, and for the more adventurous hikers, an unpaved nature trail visits the valley and creek below. For those who follow the paved trail, it winds uphill from the "egg" along the undulations of the earthwork to return to the foot of the observation tower. For any visitor, the total scene is guaranteed to be impressive.

Serpent Mound State Memorial now hosts about fifty thousand visitors each year and draws hundreds to special events throughout the year, according to site manager Beth A. Jenkins. On the second and fourth Fridays

Serpent Mound State Memorial visitors' center. *Author photo.*

of each month, an archaeologist leads a ninety-minute guided walk around Serpent Mound, giving an overview of pre-contact Native American culture in Ohio. In recent years, modern Native American tribes have celebrated large, sanctioned multiday events around the June summer solstice, featuring numerous speakers and events. Outside of Serpent Mound State Memorial, other unsanctioned community events celebrate the solstice as well.

Modern television exposure has attracted all manner of visitors, Jenkins says. The staff struggles with individuals who want to exploit the site by dancing on the effigy or tamper with the archaeology of the grounds, as well as bring crystal skulls or wear clothing of Native Americans. "People can do what they want to do," Jenkins says. "But when it comes to damaging the site or exploiting it, we've got to maintain the integrity of the site."[189]

Upcoming international events may prompt other celebrations. The effigy, already a recognized National Historic Landmark, has been nominated with eight other Native American earthwork sites by the United States Department of the Interior for inclusion as a World Heritage Site, thus making it equivalent to the Pyramids of Egypt, Stonehenge and the Great Wall of China. A decision on that application is expected shortly.

Planning your visit: Serpent Mound State Memorial is open Tuesday through Saturday 10:00 a.m. to 5:00 p.m. and Sunday noon to 5:00 p.m. It is closed Mondays. The gift shop closes at 4:30 p.m., and the site and grounds close at 5:00 p.m. Pets are welcome at Serpent Mound but must remain leashed at all times while on site. The site is closed for the following holidays/dates: Christmas Eve, Christmas Day, New Year's Eve, New Year's Day, Easter Sunday, Juneteenth, Independence Day, Thanksgiving Day, Black Friday, Memorial Day and Labor Day. There is a parking fee, waived for members of the Ohio History Connection.

The path that traces the shape around Serpent Mound is fully accessible. The site is managed by the Ohio History Connection, which can be contacted at www.OhioHistory.org.

NOTES

Prologue

1. Schmidt interview.
2. Baranoski, Schumacher, Watts and El-Saiti, "Subsurface Geology of the Serpent Mound Disturbance," 33–34; Watts, "Paleomagnetic Determination of the Age of the Serpent Mound Structure," 101–08.
3. Milam, *Guide to the Serpent Mound Impact Structure*, 22–24.

Chapter 2

4. McCulloch, "Lead Plates."
5. Mann, *Native Americans, Archaeologists & the Mounds*, 106.
6. "Historical Sketch of Adams County, Ohio."
7. "Fort Washington."
8. "Jefferson County, WV Shepherdstown in the Revolution."
9. Ohio History Connection Archives, Virginia Military District Entry Book Index.
10. Treese, *Serpent's Tale*, 5–6.
11. Wilson, "Families of Serpent Mound," 6.
12. Squire and Davis, *Ancient Monuments of the Mississippi Valley*, 262.
13. Squire and Davis, *Ancient Monuments of the Mississippi Valley*, 265.

Chapter 3

14. Wilson, "Families of Serpent Mound," 6.
15. McLean [*sic*], "Great Serpent Mound," 44.
16. Bowman, "Peabody Museum, Frederick W. Putnam," 508.
17. Putnam, "Serpent Mound of Ohio," 871.
18. Putnam, "Serpent Mound of Ohio," 872.
19. Mark, *Stranger in Her Native Land*, 141.
20. Putnam, "Serpent Mound of Ohio," 875.
21. Mark, *Stranger in Her Native Land*, 36.
22. "Bratton Township," 5.
23. Putnam, "Serpent Mound Saved," 189.
24. Ohio General Assembly, "Act Supplementary to Section 2732."

Chapter 4

25. Putnam, "Serpent Mound of Ohio," 871.
26. Romain, "In Search of Frederic W. Putnam's Serpent Mound Camp."
27. "Our Camp Life at the Serpent Mound," 8.
28. Bowman, "Peabody Museum, Frederick W. Putnam," 515.
29. "Our Camp Life at the Serpent Mound," 7.
30. "Our Camp Life at the Serpent Mound," 9.
31. "Our Camp Life at the Serpent Mound," 6; Putnam, "Serpent Mound of Ohio," 876.
32. "Our Camp Life at the Serpent Mound."
33. "Our Camp Life at the Serpent Mound."
34. "Our Camp Life at the Serpent Mound," 7.
35. "Our Camp Life at the Serpent Mound."
36. "Our Camp Life at the Serpent Mound," 11.
37. "Our Camp Life at the Serpent Mound," 18
38. "Our Camp Life at the Serpent Mound," 8.
39. "Our Camp Life at the Serpent Mound," 18.
40. Fletcher, et al., "Serpent Mound: A Fort Ancient Icon?" 113.
41. Topping, "Native American Mound Building Traditions," 238.
42. Putnam, "Serpent Mound of Ohio," 875.
43. Putnam, "Serpent Mound of Ohio," 878.
44. "Our Camp Life at the Serpent Mound," 20.
45. Putnam, "Serpent Mound of Ohio," 888.

46. Putnam, "Serpent Mound of Ohio," 871.
47. "Our Camp Life at the Serpent Mound," 13.
48. "Our Camp Life at the Serpent Mound," 15.
49. "Our Camp Life at the Serpent Mound," 21.
50. "Our Camp Life at the Serpent Mound," 18.
51. Putnam, "Serpent Mound of Ohio," 876.

Chapter 5

52. Rosenfelt, *Bratton Township*, 5.
53. Randall, *Serpent Mound*, 110.
54. *Adams County Recorder*, 282.
55. *Adams County Recorder*, 282.
56. Krupp, "New Deal, New Serpent," 60.
57. "Thirty-Fourth Annual Meeting of the Ohio State Archaeological and Historical Society," 403–04.
58. Krupp, "New Deal, New Serpent," 64.
59. Margo, "Employment and Unemployment in the 1930s," 42.
60. Kardulias, "History of Public Archaeology in Ohio," 118.
61. Krupp, "New Deal, New Serpent," 71–72.
62. Hardman and Hardman, "Map of the Great Serpent Effigy Mound," 35.
63. Hardman and Hardman, "Great Serpent and the Sun," 34.
64. Hardman and Hardman, "Great Serpent and the Sun," 36.
65. Romain, "Terrestrial Observations at the Serpent Mound," 1–19.
66. Fletcher and Cameron, "Serpent Mound: A New Look," 55.
67. Fletcher and Cameron, "Serpent Mound: A New Look," 55.
68. Fletcher, et al., "Serpent Mound: A Fort Ancient Icon?" 121–25.
69. Fletcher, et al., "Serpent Mound: A Fort Ancient Icon?" 133.
70. Lepper, "On the Age of Serpent Mound," 70.

Chapter 6

71. Willoughby, "Serpent Mound," 153–63.
72. Webb and Snow, *Adena People*, 95.
73. Mann, *Native Americans, Archaeologists & the Mounds*, 236–37.
74. Fletcher, et al., "Serpent Mound: A Fort Ancient Icon?" 138.

75. Romain, "Geometry at the Serpent Mound," 51–52.
76. Greenman, *Serpent Mound*, 3–4.
77. Herrmann, et. al., "New Multistage Construction Chronology for the Great Serpent Mound," 123.
78. Lepper, et al., "Arguments for the Age of Serpent Mound."
79. Lepper, et al., "Effigy Mounds and Rock Art," 1–46.
80. Lepper and Frolking, "Alligator Mound," 159.
81. Lepper and Frolking, "Alligator Mound," 163.
82. Mann, *Native Americans, Archaeologists & the Mounds*, 237.
83. Mann, *Spirits of Blood, Spirits of Breath*, 267n155.

Chapter 7

84. Fergusson, *Rude Stone Monuments in All Countries*, 517.
85. Mann, *Native Americans, Archaeologists & the Mounds*, 105.
86. Randall, *Serpent Mound*, 38.
87. Caldwell, *Illustrated Historical Atlas of Adams County.*
88. Allen, "Sun Symbol in Earthworks," 291.
89. Mann, *Native Americans, Archaeologists & the Mounds*, 137.
90. Mann, *Native Americans, Archaeologists & the Mounds*, 137.
91. Jefferson, *Notes on the State of Virginia*, 163.
92. Calavito, *Mound Builder Myth.*
93. Calavito, *Mound Builder Myth*, 61.
94. Pidgeon, William. *Traditions of De-Coo-Dah and Antiquarian Researches: Comparing Extensive Explorations, Surveys, and Excavations of the Wonderful and Mysterious Earthen Remains of the Mound-Builders in America.* New York: Horace Thayer 1858.
95. Calavito, *Mound Builder Myth*, 183–85, 301.
96. Squire and Davis, *Ancient Monuments of the Mississippi Valley*, 679.
97. Putnam, "Serpent Mound of Ohio," 885.
98. Putnam, "Serpent Mound of Ohio," 888.
99. Greenman, *Serpent Mound* (rev.).
100. Mills, "Excavation of the Adena Mound," 451–79.
101. Griffin, "Fort Ancient Aspect," 60.
102. Webb and Snow, *Adena People*, 341.
103. Romain, "Ancient Eclipse Paths at the Serpent Mound," 24–28.
104. Weintraub and Schwarz, "Long Shadows Over the Valley," 5.
105. Weintraub and Schwarz, "Long Shadows Over the Valley," 7.

Chapter 8

106. Hardman and Hardman, "Map of the Great Serpent Effigy Mound," 35–39.
107. Fletcher, et al., "Serpent Mound: A Fort Ancient Icon?" 133.
108. Herrmann, et al., "New Multistage Construction Chronology for the Great Serpent Mound," 117–25.
109. Haskell, *Ohio Serpent Mound.*
110. Lepper, "On the Age of Serpent Mound," 73.
111. Romain and Herrmann, "Rejoinder to Lepper Concerning Serpent Mound," 76–88.
112. Romain and Herrmann, "Rejoinder to Lepper Concerning Serpent Mound," 84–85.
113. Romain, "Serpent Mound in Its Woodland Period Context," 57–83.
114. Monaghan and Herrmann, "Serpent Mound: Still Built by the Adena," 91.
115. Lepper, "Mississippian Iconography of Serpent Mound," 49.
116. Lepper, et al., "Effigy Mounds and Rock Art," 1–46.
117. Comstock and Cook, "Climate Change and Migration Along a Mississippian Periphery," 91–108.
118. Lepper, "Why Radiocarbon Dates on Bulk Sediment from Serpent Mound Are Problematic," 1.
119. Lepper, "Great Serpent Mound and the Milky Way," 115.
120. Lepper, "Great Serpent Mound and the Milky Way," 116.
121. Lepper, "Great Serpent Mound and the Milky Way," 117.
122. Gaiter, "Eastern Shawnee Leader Reflects on the Fight for Ohio's First World Heritage Site."
123. Garner, "Reinterpretation of 'Sacred Space' at the Newark Earthworks and Serpent Mound," 94.
124. Mueller, "Earliest Occurrence of a Newly Described Domesticate in Eastern North America," 40.
125. Duncan, "Great Importance of the Great Serpent," 192–94.
126. Topping, "Native American Mound Building Traditions," 227.
127. Garner, "Reinterpretation of 'Sacred Space' at the Newark Earthworks and Serpent Mound," 93.
128. Garner, "Reinterpretation of 'Sacred Space' at the Newark Earthworks and Serpent Mound," 101.

Chapter 9

129. Richey, "Ohio's Serpent Mound," 7.
130. Mann, *Native Americans, Archaeologists & the Mounds*, 237.
131. Moroz, "Serpent's Travels, Above and Below," 2.
132. Miller, *Ancestral Mounds*, xvii.
133. Pidgeon, *Traditions of De-Coo-Dah*, 244.
134. Miller, *Ancestral Mounds*, 7.
135. Lepper, et al., "Arguments for the Age of Serpent Mound," 8.
136. Topping, "Native American Mound Building Traditions," 227.
137. Lepper, et al., "Effigy Mounds and Rock Art," 132.
138. Mann, *Spirits of Blood, Spirits of Breath*, 109–10.
139. Moroz, "Serpent's Travels, Above and Below," 7–8.
140. Hardman and Hardman, "Great Serpent and the Sun," 35.
141. Moroz, "Serpent's Travels, Above and Below," 10.
142. Davis, Burks and Abrams, "Labor Recruitment Analysis of Serpent Mound," 150.
143. Davis, Burks and Abrams, "Labor Recruitment Analysis of Serpent Mound," 151.
144. Davis, Burks and Abrams, "Labor Recruitment Analysis of Serpent Mound," 154.
145. Davis, Burks and Abrams, "Labor Recruitment Analysis of Serpent Mound," 156.

Chapter 10

146. Deloria, *Red Earth, White Lies*, 3.
147. Fine-Dare, *Grave Injustice*, 54–55.
148. Fine-Dare, *Grave Injustice*, 62
149. Fine-Dare, *Grave Injustice*, 66.
150. Fine-Dare, *Grave Injustice*, 67.
151. Babbit, "NAGPRA as a Paradigm," 67.
152. Mann, *Native Americans, Archaeologists & the Mounds*, 254–55.
153. Ferguson, "Native Americans and the Practice of Archaeology," 66.
154. Fine-Dare, *Grave Injustice*, 57.
155. Rura, "Peabody Museum Charts Progress on Repatriation."
156. Ohio History Connection, letter to Senator Brian Schwartz.
157. *American Indian Policy*, 6.

158. ProPublica, "Repatriation Database."
159. Lepper, interview.

Chapter 11

160. Putnam, "Serpent Mound of Ohio," 888.
161. Romain, "Serpent Mound: Early Interpretations," 12–13.
162. Ruth, "Moundbuilders."
163. Randall, *Serpent Mound*, 122.
164. Sanders, "Stone Serpent Mound of Boyd County," 272–84.
165. Pawlaczyk, "Did an Exploding Star Inspire Cahokians to Build Monk's Mound?"
166. Bender, "Serpent's Tale."
167. Boutet, "Great Long-Tailed Serpent."
168. Meegan, "Serpent Mound."
169. Meegan, "Serpent Mound," 7.
170. Meegan, "Serpent Mound," 12.
171. Meegan, "Serpent Mound," 10.
172. Meegan, "Serpent Mound," 20.
173. Hamilton, *Mystery of the Serpent Mound*, 7.
174. Hamilton, *Mystery of the Serpent Mound*.
175. Hamilton, *Mystery of the Serpent Mound*, xx.
176. Hamilton, *Mystery of the Serpent Mound*, 104.
177. Hamilton, *Mystery of the Serpent Mound*, 115.
178. Hamilton, *Mystery of the Serpent Mound*, 113.
179. Hamilton, *Mystery of the Serpent Mound*, 195.
180. Hamilton, *Mystery of the Serpent Mound*, 138.

Chapter 12

181. Meegan, "Serpent Mound," 6.
182. Topping, "Native American Mound Building Traditions," 238.
183. Cook, *Continuity and Change in the Native American Village*.
184. Mann, *Native Americans, Archaeologists & the Mounds*, 200.
185. Topping, "Native American Mound Building Traditions," 247.
186. "Welcome to Serpent Mound" tablet, Serpent Mound State Memorial.

187. Moroz, "Serpent's Travels, Above and Below," 11.
188. Miller, *Ancestral Mounds*, 3.

Afterword

189. Jenkins, interview.

BIBLIOGRAPHY

Adams County Recorder, vol. 69.

Allen, E.A. "The Sun Symbol in Earthworks." *The American Antiquarian and Oriental Journal* 7, no. 5 (1885).

American Indian Policy. Ohio History Connection, September 19, 2019.

Babbit, Thomaira. "NAGPRA as a Paradigm: The Historical Context and Meaning of the Native American Graves Protection and Repatriation Act." Unpublished dissertation, University of Central Oklahoma, 2011.

Baranoski, Mark T., Gregory A. Schumacher, Doyle R. Watts and Belgasem M. El-Saiti. "Subsurface Geology of the Serpent Mound Disturbance, Adams, Highland, and Pike Counties, Ohio." State of Ohio Department of Natural Resources, Columbus, Ohio, 2003.

Bender, Herman. "A Serpent's Tale: The Milky Way." Hanwakan Center for Prehistoric Astronomy, Cosmology and Cultural Landscape Studies, 2017.

Boutet, Michel-Gerald. "The Great Long-Tailed Serpent: An Iconographical Study of the Serpent in Middle Woodland Algonquin Culture." Abstract.

Bowman, David L. "The Peabody Museum, Frederic W. Putnam, and the Rise of U.S. Anthropology, 1866–1903." *American Anthropologist* 104, no. 2 (n.d.).

"Bratton Township." Adams County Heritage Center, Adams County Historical Society, 1989.

Calavito, Jason. *The Mound Builder Myth: Fake History and the Hunt for a "Lost Civilization."* University of Oklahoma Press, 2020.

Caldwell, J.A. *Illustrated Historical Atlas of Adams County*. J.A. Caldwell, 1880.

Comstock, A.R., and R.A. Cook. "Climate Change and Migration Along a Mississippian Periphery: A Fort Ancient Example." *American Antiquity* 83 (2018): 91–108.

Cook, Robert A. *Continuity and Change in the Native American Village: Multicultural Origins and Descendants of the Fort Ancient Culture*. Cambridge University Press, 2017.

Davis, Jamie L., Jarrod Burks and Elliott M. Abrams. "Labor Recruitment Analysis of Serpent Mound, Ohio." In *Architectural Energetics in Archaeology: Analytical Expansions and Global Explorations*, edited by Leah McCurdy and Elliott M. Abrams. Routledge, 2019.

Deloria, Vine, Jr. *Red Earth, White Lies: Native Americans and the Myth of Scientific Fact*. Fulcrum Publishing, 1997.

Duncan, James R. "The Great Importance of the Great Serpent." In *Explanations in Iconography: Ancient American Indian Art, Symbol and Meaning*, edited by Carol Diaz-Granados. Oxbow Books, 2023.

Ferguson, T.J. "Native Americans and the Practice of Archaeology." *Annual Review of Anthropology* 25 (1996).

Fergusson, James. *Rude Stone Monuments in All Countries; Their Age and Uses*. John Murray, Albemarle Street, 1872.

Fine-Dare, Kathleen. *Grave Injustice: The American Indian Repatriation Movement and NAGPRA*. University of Nebraska Press, 2002.

Fletcher, Robert, and Terry Cameron. "Serpent Mound: A New Look at an Old Snake-in-the-Grass." *Ohio Archaeologist* 38, no. 1 (Winter 1988).

Fletcher, Robert V., Terry L. Cameron, Bradley T. Lepper, Dee Anne Wymer and William Pickard. "Serpent Mound: A Fort Ancient Icon?" *Midcontinental Journal of Archaeology* 21, no. 1 (Spring 1996).

"Fort Washington." American Battlefield Trust. www.Battlefields.org.

Gaiter, Chris. "Eastern Shawnee Leader Reflects on the Fight for Ohio's First World Heritage Site." *Columbus Monthly*, January 8, 2024. ColumbusMonthly.com.

Garner, Sandra. "Reinterpretation of 'Sacred Space' at the Newark Earthworks and Serpent Mound: Settler Colonialism and Discourses of 'Sacred.'" *Review of International American Studies* 16, no. 1 (Spring–Summer 2023).

Greenman, Emerson. *Serpent Mound.* Ohio Historical Society, 1925.

———. *Serpent Mound.* Rev. ed. Ohio Historical Society, 1970.

Hamilton, Ross. *The Mystery of the Serpent Mound: In Search of the Alphabet of the Gods*. Frog Ltd., 2001.

Hardman, Clark, and Marjorie F. Hardman. "The Great Serpent and the Sun." *Ohio Archaeologist* 37, no. 3 (Fall 1987).

———. "A Map of the Great Serpent Effigy Mound." *Ohio Archaeologist* 37, no. 1 (Winter 1987).

Haskell, Jon R. *Ohio Serpent Mound: An Analysis of Two Unreported Motifs in North American Indigenous Art*. Indigenous Peoples Research Foundation, 2016.

Herrmann, Edward G., G. William Monaghan, William F. Romain, Timothy M. Schilling, Jarrod Burks, Karen L. Leone, Matthew P. Purtill and Alan C. Tonetti. "A New Multistage Construction Chronology for the Great Serpent Mound, USA." *Journal of Archaeological Science* 50 (2014).

"Historical Sketch of Adams County, Ohio." *Caldwell's Historical Atlas of Adams County, Ohio*. J.A. Caldwell, 1880.

"Jefferson County, WV Shepherdstown in the Revolution." West Virginia Genealogy Trails, Appendix A.

Jefferson, Thomas. *Notes on the State of Virginia*. John Stockdale, 1787.

Jenkins, Beth A. Interview, August 1, 2024.

Jerrell, Jason, and Sarah Farmer. *Ages of the Giants: A Cultural History of the Tall Ones in Prehistoric America*. Serpent Mound Books and Press, 2017.

Kardulias, P. Nick. "A History of Public Archaeology in Ohio." *Ohio History* 98 (1989).

Krupp, Rory. "New Deal, New Serpent: Public Works Projects at Serpent Mound State Memorial." *Journal of Ohio Archaeology* 7 (2020).

Lepper, Bradley T. "The Great Serpent Mound and the Milky Way." *Journal of Skyscape Archaeology* 8 (2022).

———. Interview, September 27, 2024.

———. "The Mississippian Iconography of Serpent Mound." *Journal of Ohio Archaeology* 7 (2020).

———. "On the Age of Serpent Mound: A Reply to Romain and Colleagues." *Midcontinental Journal of Archaeology* 43, no. 1 (Spring 2018).

———. "Why Radiocarbon Dates on Bulk Sediment from Serpent Mound Are Problematic." *Current Research in Ohio Archaeology* (2020).

Lepper, Bradley T., and Tod A. Frolking. "Alligator Mound: Geoarchaeological and Iconographical Interpretations of a Late Prehistoric Effigy Mound in Central Ohio, USA." *Cambridge Archaeological Journal* 13, no. 2 (2003).

Lepper, Bradley T., James R. Duncan, Carol Diaz-Granados and Tod A. Frolking. "Arguments for the Age of Serpent Mound." *Cambridge Archaeological Journal* (2018). www.cambridge.org/core.

Lepper, Bradley T., Robert Boszhardt, James R. Duncan and Carol Diaz-Granados. "Effigy Mounds and Rock Art of Midcontinental North America: Shared Iconography, Shared Stories." *North American Archaeologist* 43, no. 1 (2021).

———. "Effigy Mounds and Rock Art of Midcontinental North America: Shared Iconography, Shared Stories." In *Explanations in Iconography: Ancient American Indian Art, Symbol, and Meaning*, edited by Carol Diaz-Granado. Oxbow Books, 2023.

Mann, Barbara Alice. *Native Americans, Archaeologists & the Mounds*. Peter Lang Publishing, 2003.

———. *Spirits of Blood, Spirits of Breath: The Twinned Cosmos of Indigenous America*. Oxford University Press, 2016.

Margo, Robert A. "Employment and Unemployment in the 1930s." *Journal of Economic Perspectives* 7, no. 2 (Spring 1993).

Mark, Joan. *A Stranger in Her Native Land: Alice Fletcher and the Native Americans*. University of Nebraska Press, 1988.

McCulloch, Delta A. "The Lead Plates." In West Virginia Archives & History, "Celeron de Blainville Buries Lead Plates." *Pocahontas Times*, November 20, 1924.

McLean [*sic*], J.P. "The Great Serpent Mound." *The American Antiquarian and Oriental Journal* 7, no. 1 (January 1885).

Meegan, William John. "Serpent Mound: An American Indian Mystery School." academia.edu.

Milam, Keith A. *Guide to the Serpent Mound Impact Structure, South-Central Ohio*. Ohio Department of Natural Resources, Division of Geological Survey, 2016, 22–24.

Miller, Jay. *Ancestral Mounds: Vitality and Volatility of Native America.* University of Nebraska Press, 2015.

Mills, W.C. "Excavation of the Adena Mound." *Ohio Archaeological and Historical Society Quarterly* 10 (1901).

Monaghan, G. William, and Edward W. Herrmann. "Serpent Mound: Still Built by the Adena, and Still Rebuilt During the Fort Ancient Period." *Midcontinental Journal of Archaeology* 44, no. 1 (2019).

Moroz, Charlotte. "The Serpent's Travels, Above and Below." Pacifica Graduate Institute doctoral research paper, 2022.

Mueller, Natalie. "The Earliest Occurrence of a Newly Described Domesticate in Eastern North America: Adena/Hopewell Communities and Agricultural Innovation." *Journal of Anthropological Archaeology* 49 (2018).

Ohio General Assembly. "An Act Supplementary to Section 2732 of the Revised Statutes of Ohio." Section 1.

Ohio History Connection Archives. Virginia Military District Entry Book Index, 1787–1852.

Ohio History Connection, letter to Senator Brian Schwartz, June 16, 2023, on compliance with NAGPRA. Ohio State Archives Series 4494, GR 8046-8049.

"Our Camp Life at the Serpent Mound, July and August 1889." Manuscript, Ohio History Archives, Cultural History and Anthropology Box 27.

Pawlaczyk, George. "Did an Exploding Star Inspire Cahokians to Build Monk's Mound?" *Belleville News-Democrat*, July 16, 2018.

Pidgeon, William. *Traditions of De-Coo-Dah and Antiquarian Researches: Comparing Extensive Explorations, Surveys, and Excavations of the Wonderful and Mysterious Earthen Remains of the Mound-Builders in America*. Horace Thayer, 1858.

ProPublica. "The Repatriation Database: Ohio History Connection (formerly the Ohio Historical Society)." www.projects.propublica.org./repatriation.

Putnam, F.W. "The Serpent Mound Saved." *Ohio History Journal* 1, no. 2 (September 1887): 189.

Putnam, Frederic Ward. "The Serpent Mound of Ohio." *Century Magazine* 39 (1889/1890).

Randall, E.O. *The Serpent Mound, Adams County, Ohio: Mystery of the Mound and History of the Serpent.* Ohio State Archaeological and Historical Society, 1907.

Richey, Clifford C. "Ohio's Serpent Mound and Its Relationship to Venus." *Depicted Sign Language: An Ancient System of Communication*, 2022. Academia.edu.

Romain, William F. "Ancient Eclipse Paths at the Serpent Mound." *Ohio Archaeologist* 38, no. 4 (Fall 1988).

———. "Geometry at the Serpent Mound." *Ohio Archaeologist* 38, no. 1 (Winter 1988).

———. "In Search of Frederic W. Putnam's Serpent Mound Camp." Academia.edu.

———. "Serpent Mound: Early Interpretations." 2022. Academia.edu.

———. "Serpent Mound in Its Woodland Period Context: Second Rejoinder to Lepper." *Midcontinental Journal of Archaeology* 44, no. 1 (Spring 2019).

———. "Terrestrial Observations at the Serpent Mound." *Ohio Archaeologist* 38, no. 2 (Spring 1988).

Romain, William F., and Edward Herrmann. "Rejoinder to Lepper Concerning Serpent Mound." *Midcontinental Journal of Archaeology* 43, no. 1 (n.d).

Rosenfelt, Alice. Adams County Heritage Center. *Bratton Township*. Adams County Historical Society, 1989.

Rura, Nicole. "Peabody Museum Charts Progress on Repatriation: NAGPRA Project Staff Doubled to Support Three-Year Commitment for Consultation, Return of All Ancestors and Associated Funerary Belongings." *Harvard Gazette*, October 26, 2023. News.Harvard.edu.

Ruth, Susan. "The Moundbuilders." In *Archaeology*, ch. 9. *Open Educational Textbook.* Central New Mexico Community College, 2023.

Sanders, Sara. "The Stone Serpent Mound of Boyd County, Kentucky: An Investigation of a Stone Effigy Structure." *Midcontinental Journal of Archaeology* 16, no. 2 (1991).

Schmidt, David. Interview, October 21, 2022.

Squire, Ephraim, and E.G. Davis. *Ancient Monuments of the Mississippi Valley*. Smithsonian Institution, 1848.

"Thirty-Fourth Annual Meeting of the Ohio State Archaeological and Historical Society." *Ohio Archaeological and Historical Society Journal* 28, no. 4 (October 1919).

Topping, Peter. "Native American Mound Building Traditions." In *Round Mounds and Monumentality in the British Neolithic and Beyond*, edited by Peter Topping, J. Leary, T. Darvill and D. Field. Oxbow Books, 2010.

Treese, Lorett. *A Serpent's Tale: Discovering America's Ancient Mound Builders.* Westholme Publishing, 2016.

Watts, D.R. "Paleomagnetic Determination of the Age of the Serpent Mound Structure." *Ohio Journal of Science* 104, no. 4 (2004).

Webb, William S., and Charles Snow. *The Adena People.* Vol. 1. University of Kentucky Department of Anthropology and Archaeology, 1945.

Webb, William S., and Raymond S. Baby. *The Adena People.* Vol. 2. University of Kentucky Department of Anthropology and Archaeology, 1957.

Weintraub, Daniel, and Kevin R. Schwarz. "Long Shadows Over the Valley: Findings from ASC Group's Excavations at Serpent Mound State Memorial." *Current Research in Ohio Archaeology* (2013).

Willoughby, Charles C. "The Serpent Mound of Adams County, Ohio." *American Anthropologist* 21, no. 2 (April–June 1919).

Wilson, Delsey. "The Families of Serpent Mound." *Our Heritage* 44, no. 1 (Spring–Summer 2022).

———. Interview, March 13, 2023.

ABOUT THE AUTHOR

I first encountered Serpent Mound when, as a public relations writer for the Ohio Historical Society, I had several occasions to explore the site. Since then, I had the opportunity to return as a tourist a couple times until a few years ago, when site manager Beth Jenkins mentioned a real need to have an up-to-date book for guests. Having just completed another Ohio history tale, I took the bait and entered into a fascinating study of one extraordinary place and many formerly misunderstood cultures that we are only now beginning to understand.

My formal interest in history dates to my days as a newspaper reporter, when I followed a reader's tip and discovered the background of a family cemetery where a veteran of the War of 1812 rests with other members of his family felled in a cholera epidemic of around 1830. I followed that with employment in the Ohio Historical Society and then graduate studies including historiography, the formalized study of history. As a college associate professor, I studied the Wright brothers' photography in preparation for publications and presentations at the 100th anniversary of the first flight.

I am now a professor emeritus in the Department of Communication at Wright State University, where I taught journalism courses for twenty-nine years. In 2009, I coauthored a true-crime book about the 1946 murder of a Xenia police officer and its aftermath, and since retiring in 2015, I have written a short science-fiction novel and then a book about the rebuilding of Ohio's National Road with prison labor during World War I.

I continue to teach seminars for the University of Dayton Osher Lifelong Learning Institute, including two "What Is News?" seminars, two "Journalism in the Cinema" seminars, "Jesus of Nazareth as Seen by Scholars" and, in 2024, "The Mysterious Mounds: What Are They? Who Built Them and Why?" As to formal education, I earned a PhD in mass communication and master's degree in visual communication, with minors in film studies, from Ohio University, and I earned a bachelor of science degree in journalism from Bowling Green State University. A Dayton-area native, my wife, Karin Avila-John, and I live in Kettering, Ohio.